The Violet Light

THE POWER THAT CHANGES EVERYTHING

Paco Alarcon – *Kahan*

authorHOUSE

1663 LIBERTY DRIVE, SUITE 200
BLOOMINGTON, INDIANA 47403
(800) 839-8640
www.authorhouse.com

First published by AuthorHouse 02/24/05

ISBN: 1-4184-5029-4 (Paperback)
ISBN: 1-4184-5028-6 (Dust Jacket)

Library of Congress Control Number: 2003095860
This book is printed on acid free paper.

Printed in the United States of America
Bloomington, IN

A Course in Miracles quotes,
copyright: Foundation for A Course in Miracles.
In order of appearance:
Text Book:
Chapter 12, VI, 1
Exercise Book:
Lesson 169, title & 2, 1
Lesson 116, title, 1
Lesson 344, title.

Cover idea – Kahan
Cover design – Dolphin Press

This book is offered to God Source.

It is dedicated to Jesus,
To the Spirit of God in the Violet Light
To the Divine Self in each one…
…and it is offered for the freedom of all.

"I would ask the genii of the magic lamp for one wish: Grant me your powers."

"Everything is possible for he who believes."

– Jesus, The Gospels

"Everything is possible for he who believes in the power of love."

– Kahan

THE AMOUNT OF LOVE YOU CAN TRANSMIT

IS THE SAME AS THE AMOUNT OF YOURSELF,

YOU HAVE SURRENDERED TO LOVE.

IT IS THE AMOUNT OF LOVE YOU HAVE EMBRACED

THE AMOUNT OF LETTING GO YOU HAVE ENDURED,

HOW MUCH YOU HAVE EMPTIED YOURSELF.

IN THAT SPACE LOVE LIVES FREELY

THIS IS WHAT BRINGS YOU JOY.

AS YOU STOP FIGHTING GOD,

YOU KNOW THE BLISS OF FREEDOM.

YOU THEN UNDERSTAND PEACE IN UNITY

AS THE WAY OF GOD.

MOTIVES CEASE AND YOU ARE ABSORBED

IN THE OCEAN OF LOVE.

THE HEART CANNOT BE KNOWN WITH THE MIND,

ONE MUST SURRENDER TO THE PRESENCE

OF GOD IN THE HEART.

THIS IS LOVE.

– Kahan

GRATITUDE

•

All my love and gratitude to all the family of the Violet Light across the world. With your loving smiles and bright eyes full of joy and gratitude in receiving the Violet Light, you have given me so much purpose. Seeing your transformations before my eyes, you have given me faith and vision to see there is much more to do for so many. You have shown me as your hearts opened at the touch of this light, more of what this light is about. Seeing you, I have seen humanity as a whole. This book is also for you and for all those yet to come to the Violet Light.

I want to deeply thank all the people that have answered the call of the Violet Light in their hearts, and have become part of this story of love, freedom and evolution as members of the family of light of our beloved planet Earth. My gratitude also to the people that have contributed to this book so openly with their experiences.

I thank Mexico deeply with all my love for being such a sacred land, and for providing me with the perfect circumstances for the connection with this divine light.

•

My deepest gratitude and love to Jesus who has made it all possible answering my call immediately with the Violet Light. With profound gratitude to my spiritual sister Thelma de Leon, who produced the spark in me that made me intensify my connection with Jesus, resulting in this connection with the light.

I am deeply grateful to Marian Espi Lluch and the group of the Violet Light in Spain, for keeping the meditations for Earth peace with the

Violet Light alive, while I was traveling taking the light to people and getting the book ready.

Very special thanks to Valerie Badgett for her excellent suggestion on creating the common concerns section, which has turned out to be one of the jewels of the book. Also gratitude and love to all those around the world, especially in Mexico, Spain and the US who have supported my work with the Violet Light – your service has provided unlimited blessings to humanity and the Earth.

Very special gratitude to my Mother who has supported me and therefore my work in so many wonderful ways.

My profound gratitude and love to all my spiritual teachers who have done so much for me, helping me with my evolution and allowing me to take myself to where I am and do what I do. Your many blessings have been the road I have traveled on. This book is filled with them. My most profound gratitude to God Himself, who has allowed it all to happen with the unmistakable Grace of His presence. I bow in silence, my hands together to reach where words can't in total gratitude and awe at the greatness of God's Love... and at that magical way in which it manifests as the Violet Light.

♥

Contents

Chapter 12
Activation – Part II: Integrating The Light In You

Chapter 13
Practices: How To Change Your Life And The World

Chapter 14
A Guide To Life's Path: The Principles Of The Violet Light

FOREWORD

"Since the beginning of time the human being has had light within. It is the light of his being – the light of his Creator. The love of God cannot be measured – one can only experience it, be it, by knowing this light. It is so big and immense that if you could really have a glimpse of what it is, your joy and liberation would be so great that it would change your vision of life and of the Universe for all eternity. This light of life and power is testimony of the love of God. God has given Himself completely to His creation, putting Himself in it giving Man all that He is. There cannot be greater love than that of He, who having all, gives all to what He creates – to the life He has created so that it has life.

The human being does not understand his Creator, and has not embraced His offering. God is at your service. You, not having realized you have all because He has given it to you – those "Divine Gifts" – look for your satisfaction in acquiring for your body and your mind, for your senses and desires, possessions and ephemeral experiences and satisfactions, that always leave you dissatisfied. When inside you there is the most incredible treasure you could ever have dreamed of.

You have created a world of idols – of dependencies and illusions – looking for that lost power, that love that fulfils you. Idols of power, joy, hope, wealth, love ... idols of loneliness, unhappiness, suffering, fear, pain, separation, madness, and you worship them in spite of yourself believing that in them, there is something for you, some salvation, something that makes your life better, more bearable and that gives it more sense without really realizing that every time you turn around, they betray you. You look for The Holy Grail – The Ark of The Covenant – The Challis of Salvation.

No my brother, my sister, that is not the way. The Holy Grail is inside you. The Ark, is the Ark of the Covenant between you and God, a covenant truly eternal with the Creator, with life and light – in your divine light inside. No treasure of this world will give you eternal life. Thus, you search for temporary crumbs of joy in the idols you have created, in the hope that they will last a little longer: a time of deception that ends with empty hands and a closed heart. This will only take you to madness. It will never satiate you because in the depth of your being, you know that permanent joy does exist and also eternal life. Hence you look for them. But searching for them in the wrong place won't give them you. However much adoration you offer them, this will never turn your idols into bearers of joy and abundance.

Why do you close your eyes every time to embrace an idol to save you, to find yourself scratched and broken on the ground in a sudden awakening? Insistence on the wrong won't make it right. So you go around in circles stepping on the same ground. The light brings the spiral upwards – it breaks the circle, moves you out. Take it.

God is more than what has been described ever, and hence He sends His sweet but firm hand to rescue you, offering you His Grace for you to discover His gifts. His radiant love in His spirit of light, arrives now to open the door that you closed. Open this door as the ones you will find here have opened it and discover within you, what has already been given to you. I, with the Brothers of the light, bring you this offering of Light of the Spirit of God. Receive it openly. It will change your life and your existence. Open the door to the cave of your inner treasures. God sends you a spiritual light of His Grace, for you to live your earthly life in heaven. Discover this divine gift without precedent. God offers it to you with all His love.

What has been called the Light of The Seventh Ray, comes to transform your vision and that of each one on this Earth forever. Seize intensely this divine ship towards a new world of light, love, peace and power, free of shadows, free of idols, free of sin. I give testimony of it. You will never have to go back.

This Violet Light of the Divine Alchemy that has blessed everything without limits wherever it has arrived, is now at your feet. This is the gift of God for you and for your brothers and sisters now.

This is your time here and now. Learn and understand how to live your life in the light that is given to you. Don't you already yearn for a real change? True peace? Unconditional love? Light without shadows? Take a step, we are waiting for you there, where life is thus lived. Substitute your idols for this light and you will find the joy you are looking for. Know in the spiritual light now available, the love that will satiate all your dreams. I have not brought this light for a few. I have brought it for many. Include yourself in the sharing. We all here support your happiness, your evolution and your freedom constantly.

Know, as I have known, the immense and infinite glory of the Divine in you, exploring your Inner Universe, discovering the light of the divine gifts that He has given you.

Make no mistake, this is the one who says it is.

With the blessings of God's love.
Your brother in the light."

Jesus

INTRODUCTION

"Accept the only truth that divine joy is your deserved reality without conditions. You do not have to become anything, nor sanctify yourself for it. It is the communion with it what sanctifies. Set aside the puerile illusions that the saint is a special being, arriving at sanctity through own merits. His only merit is to have realized that fact and to have embraced the complete joy of the Divine in him... to have accepted liberation where it is."

—Jesus

My aim with this book is to start a consciousness revolution on the planet at all levels. A revolution that has as main objective to make anyone spiritually independent.

This process is inevitable. The moment people are put in touch with this energy, their lives start to change. They start to improve and to move in the right direction. Their spirituality acquires new dimensions and they find a new freedom. It could not be any other way: higher vibrations rule over lower vibrations and this energy is the highest vibration of Universal Intelligence.

This revolution is taking people to the realization that, to change, prosper and be happy it is not necessary to suffer. I mean here to endure hardship. This will be proved to everyone who chooses to take a step in the direction proposed here. The only suffering is the one you might bring up as your ego reacts to God's power and blessings. Soon we all learn it is best to surrender and let God do His work in restoring our consciousness to unity, love and peace.

This energy is powerful, it is available to you and it will change your life. All you have to do is work with it. I will lead you to the connection with this precious gift of the Creator. The rest is up to the energy. I don't include you in the equation of success because it does not depend on you. Success is guaranteed because, here, it is independent of human condition. The energy will do its work on you regardless of your understanding of it, or of your qualifications. To change your life with this energy you do not need to understand deep spiritual matters. You only need to connect with it. You do not have to figure out how it works. You get the benefits independently. You just connect as the book will show you and everything will happen for you. I understand this is a very different perspective from the one most human beings have been taught. But it is the way it is.

Think of the life you want, what you would like to see in it, how you would like to feel… It is all available here. This is about how to bring a very high spiritual energy down to your life, and experiencing all that it implies in practical terms. This is the way your vision can be made real. And it can be made real now, not in the future or in another lifetime. We are talking of making things happen in present time. The Violet Light accelerates time so much that brings the future to the present thus collapsing time. This is why with it we can talk about the power of miracle. A miracle is a collapse of time.

The energy of the Violet Light connects you directly with the Divine Source of life. Then all Grace, Light, and Power are accessible to you. Then you start to live your spiritual independence. We all need a connection that allows us to hook on to the main power of light, bliss and love of the Universe. The energy of the Violet Light presented in this work, does this for you. It reveals the power of the Universe in you. It is within you, once tapped you go there for recharging, healing, understanding, resurrecting, for Grace transforms you. This is the Grace of the Violet Light.

We are superconscious beings – each of us a huge being of energy and light that is anchored to this body. But we only have awareness of the personality part, the smallest part of us, the part that fits into the body. We need to access the rest of our being. We have to go there to find true confidence and power. They are not in the personality or the body. If you go to them to find that confidence and power, the power there will always let you down. That is why things don't work as they should, because we are looking for them in the personality sphere. Contacting our higher consciousness is the resurrection we are all looking for. This is the way your being, your life resurrects from mediocrity: you access the extraordinary in you.

We absorb the energy to which we are exposed. So we want to be exposed to the highest energies available, which give us true love and power, those energies which raise our frequency so that we access the totality of our being. Then the fun starts: anything is possible.

We have a contracted awareness. The Violet Light expands it for us. Then we have access to all our higher energy; we activate our love power, our highest power and love that then become available to change our lives.

•

Spirituality is not just for people looking for a greater meaning of life, it is for everyone. The spiritual sphere of life is the one that holds all the secrets to the real working of all things. While many people want to believe there is nothing beyond what is perceived by the senses, others find in Spirit the treasures the rest look for where they can never be found. This energy is not for spiritual people, it is for everyone. There is not such thing as spiritual people. There are only people, and we are all spiritual. Some know it; some prefer to ignore it. This energy is for everyone because it has the power to benefit the life of every human being immensely – whoever you are, wherever you are at. When I was getting the book ready I did not want to define a specific target group for it. I always said: "This light is for everyone on the planet." So the work here is designed to take you from your inexistent, basic or advanced level of spirituality, further along the way to experience your spiritual independence, the greatness of your own life and of the Universe.

You, as a human being, should know what is going on in here. Because if you are human, the solution to everything in yourself and in your life is given here. I cannot say this is the only place you will find it, because that is not true. But I can say this is a place where you will find spiritual energy available, in such a practical and accessible way and with such potency, that will make the spiritual experience so available to you that it will transform your life.

•

After years of intense spiritual work, I developed a strong connection with the highest spiritual planes. I reached the Violet Light through a great deal of spiritual preparation. In this way I was able to receive it, understand it and anchor it to my energy field so that I could pass it along, with the help of my supporting team in the Light. So the good news is that you don't have to spend years working spiritually to access it. It can be made available to you immediately. I have done the work; you receive the benefits. This is my job, to make this Grace and Power available to you.

If you are involved with a spiritual practice, put Violet Light into it. This will greatly enhance it. If you meditate, surround yourself with Violet Light as you do it. If you go to a specific church and pray there, visualize Violet Light around you and others as you pray. See the world surrounded with Violet Light. You can also include in your Life any of the Violet Light meditations presented here. I strongly recommend you do, having seen the miraculous results in so many people over the years.

If you are a Christian, a Buddhist, a Muslim, a Taoist, a follower of Hindu religion, or if you don't believe in God, this energy will help you equally in realizing the full potential of what you are. You need not change religion. Whatever it is you do, put Violet Light into it, this will give it a great boost. This energy is open to all. In my courses and workshops, I have had people from many nationalities and religious backgrounds. It has worked for them all.

You should know that the Violet Light is already in you. It is part of your main Inner Light. The soul has this energy in it. The Violet Light here activates that divine light already in you, to help you access your divine potential. Our inner light is a seed of divine potentiality that needs to be fully activated.

●

In a World of big powers where it seems so inaccessible for us to influence things, we now have a tremendous power to affect life and its outcomes at all levels, without changing our daily lives. We have the power of God in our hands working with us through a light, which we can use to positively affect the world and ourselves.

With this light you have nothing to lose, except your limitations – and you have everything to win. With the Violet Light you are going to do the same you are doing now. Your life will look the same from the outside, but your experience of being alive will be greatly transformed. That which you do, will feel different. Your sense of priorities will change and what is important to you inside, will come to the front. You will illumine all and bring life to everything with your own light.

●

When I asked Jesus to take me to his highest teaching, his answer was the Violet Light. I had been working on my spiritual development for more than fifteen years, and although I had been rooted in inner peace and powerful transformations had taken place, I have never felt so blessed in my life. The Violet Light that Jesus put me in contact with, has changed my life and myself completely. To him and to this divine light I owe my experience of life in joy, in true power and in love. I have discovered what I have called: "true prosperity," which is far beyond material success, but includes it and promotes it, in an experience of life bountiful at all levels, in which the power of love guides me in the form of this high vibration of light, which has the power to change everything for the best. Even the things that we might think will never change, will surrender to the power of love of the Violet Light. Our most cherished visions about life stop being dreams in the hands of this energy.

This has been my personal experience and that of the many that have been touched by this light. I have witnessed their changes, their rejuvenation, their shinning light, the miracles in their lives and their tears of gratitude and relief, as they were finally freed from struggling and limitations, but most of all, from the contracting ego experience of themselves, to go on to live in an expanded state of joy and peace that is not of this Earth, but the Violet Light is making it so.

I encourage you to try it for yourself. Give yourself this opportunity. You will never look back.

Paco Alarcon
San Rafael, California
April 2003

●

"Whatever you are doing in your life,

whatever spiritual path or religion you are following,

don't change it, it is your treasure.

Just paint it with Violet Light."

A MESSAGE TO READERS

As you work with this energy, your evolutional and personal processes will be accelerated. You are being liberated from great burdens and contractions in yourself. This is a blessing. You are taken to a new place where you can experience greater love and power.

These processes are ones that you will have to go through anyway, regardless of this light. They are the growing ways you have to face in your life. The Violet Light will compact them for you, and your processes will manifest sooner, faster, and more easily than what it would be without the light. So you are freed from restrictions blocking your path. This means that for many of the good things awaiting you in your life, you don't have to wait longer. God is working. His power and love are being activated in you and in your life. You can resist the process and have a difficult time, or you can let go of the old as you open up and flow. The new reality unfolding for you contains greater energy and happiness. Through difficult periods of change, remember where you are going – don't lose perspective. Take distance from your ego negative reactions. Resistance causes you pain. You are being freed as the old is being removed from you. Choose to follow the path of love, instead of the path of pain. Hold to your center. The way of the light is a greater way. Don't forget you are being helped in a way you may not recognize at that moment.

If you want true freedom, there is no other way.
Have faith. God is supporting you completely.

ABOUT THE VIOLET FLAME

The Violet Energy has been known for many years as "The Violet Flame." This flame is one of the forms of the Violet Light. At this time the Violet Light is coming with more power. It contains higher frequencies of light capable of changing individual and collective realities, at a speed unknown on the Earth until now. It has the ability to burn karmas at great speed and to resurrect the Christ Consciousness – Divine Self – in everyone. It makes everything work. If it is not going to work, it dissolves it and replaces it with a better reality. The reports from people that have known the Flame and have received this connection with the Violet Light, are all the same: it is very different from what they previously knew. The first emanation of the light did a tremendous amount of work here, getting everything ready for this emanation that comes to finish the work. It is doing it at such speed, with such excellence and impeccability that it really has the signature of God Himself. It has left us all astonished. As Saint Germain said originally about this energy: "It is the mere presence of God acting."

ABOUT NAMING GOD

When addressing God, I will use "He." He is very personal to all. So I want to avoid saying "It" or having to say "He" and "She" all the time. God has no gender. God has no attributes. He just Is. When He manifests Himslef, the manifestation develops as feminine and masculine, Yin and Yang polarities and principles. But at source, He is One. So I will refer to God as "He" always, meaning Its totality: "He" "She" "It" and "All".
Oneness.

The Story

During the month of September 1997 something unexpected happened to me, that changed my life beyond imagination. At that time I was called into meditation by Jesus. In his presence and in meditation, he transmitted to me the teaching and consciousness of a spiritual energy that had an amazing vibration and an incredible color: The Violet Light.

This happened in constant encounters and meditations in which he radiated The Violet Light to me, and gave me instructions on how to meditate, and how to connect with The Violet Light. I spent hours daily in meditation for almost a month. This process culminated when he said that I was ready and that the transformation had taken place.

During that time, even outside of meditation I found myself immersed in an ocean of Violet Light in which I felt protected, happy and blessed. When I started to take to people some of the teachings and meditations he had shown me, to my surprise the miracle started to manifest: they were having the same experience I had. This spiritual energy, until then unknown to me, was helping people find inner peace, dissolve their karmas and making their lives work.

Little did I know then of the full transcendence of all I had received. But it was clear the path to follow: I knew I had to dedicate my life to bringing this energy to people. It has been a blessing to see so many over the years, being transformed like me into more happy liberated people, filled with gratitude, their souls expanded in this light and their lives blessed beyond imagination. After the period of my initiation, the essence of the teachings has been expanded to create a complete system for the evolution of the human consciousness, and for the ascension of mankind. The information and practices related to the energy were structured in three courses that gave the teachings, but most importantly, they gave the inner spiritual experience of the Violet Light: a total transformation of people's inner and outer lives.

This wonderful experience, energy and teachings of many years have generated this book, so that the liberation and empowerment this energy offers is also available to everyone in this way. For the purpose of seeing many more in that state of grace, is why I write it. Here it is for everyone to discover this immense treasure.

May this work of love open the door to millions to receive the Grace of God in this way.

HOW THE BOOK WORKS ON YOU

As you read the book through the chapters, the Light will enter you and do its work. Your light frequencies will be awakened. Deep in you, there are codes of light that hold the secrets of your life and evolution. As you read and follow the steps provided, The Violet Light will activate them. Don't expect to understand the workings of the energy. Just let go, and let it happen. The energy of The Violet Light is right now with you.

"You are not reading mere words, you are reading energy."

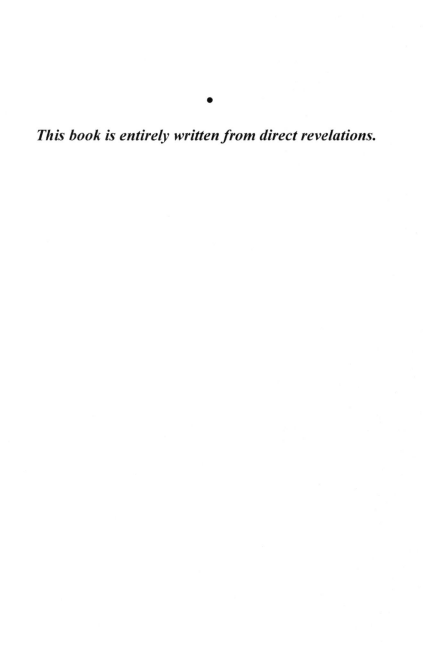

This book is entirely written from direct revelations.

PART I

THE COMPLETE OVERVIEW

"God has given us all.
It is the moment to go inside
and find it.
Then live it and offer it to others
and to God Himself."

– K a h a n

– CHAPTER 1 –

•

THE VIOLET LIGHT:
A NEW KIND OF LOVE POWER

"Love is the only real thing."
– The Ascended Masters

Mankind believes it doesn't have everything, hence its unending search after gain. The truth is far from that: Man has a true wealth of treasures within himself. This book presents a key to open your treasure chest of divine gifts and true abundance, through the activation of the power of love that is inside you. This key is The Violet Light. This light removes the blockages that impede you to see that God has given you all. It is fundamental in your change towards a greater life, to realize that God has already given you what you are looking for.

Every human being has light within, and everyone must activate it. Only when this inner light is fully active, things work properly in our lives and we access all our potential. The divine gifts are in this light. When this inner light is active, you access all the divine gifts. Until then you are not embracing all the power God has given you. The power that has to be awakened in Man is the "Love Power." This happens through the activation of the light inside.

"Light is love with power and power with love."

When your inner light is active, the power of love is working in you and everything happens for you. This is not the love we know here, but love as the cosmic force that creates everything and makes it all happen. So if you want things to happen in your life, you need to

3

activate this power of love activating your light inside. This book is about that.

God has already given you all. It is time to become conscious of the infinite treasure you have been given. Through a wrong belief system that tells humanity the opposite, people look for plenitude outside. Then pray to God for His bounty. This is the wrong prayer. God has already fulfilled His part. The right prayer should be:

"Dear God, show me what you have given me.
Remove my veils of ignorance so that
I see, I recognize your gifts in me,
so that I use them for my blessing and
the blessing of others and of all life."

God has put everything in the heart of Man. But Man has not gone there to find it. The heart is the door to all the secrets you are looking for. God's love is the key to opening it. It is called Grace. The Violet Light is a form of this Grace. It allows you to access all the love power of God in the heart.

In life, things work well for a while, then things stop working. And nobody is really questioning why this is happening. It has been commonly accepted that this is the way, and all have to try their best. This is not the truth. This is the belief of people who do not have their inner light active, and who therefore do not access all of what they are and all they have available to them: power, love, wisdom unlimited. When there is access to light, things work and we and our lives evolve.

If you are not conscious of your potentialities, you are not capable of living life fully. You want to experience freedom, inner peace. These can only be obtained when you are in conscious possession of the divine gifts. We are all full of divine gifts. The activation of our light is the activation of those gifts. The Violet Light activates your inner light to give you access to all those divine gifts, reestablishing the direct connection with your Universal Supply Source. What Man is

4

really looking for is the love power of the soul – that loving energy that makes everything work.

"You need to free your soul power"

The heart is the temple of this power; we must go there. The Violet Light energy provides the opening of this temple in a new way, as it casts aside and gets rid of all the thick overgrowth that hides the access to the temple. Then it blasts the doors open and goes in to ignite the power of love contained within the soul. This is the gift that we are given in these times of change and immense evolution: a fast way into the power source of our lives.

The soul of Man in the heart needs to be freed. For this the doors of the heart have to be opened through the purification of our negative energies. Those energies are blocking the heart keeping the soul in a prison, away from our consciousness where we cannot touch the Divine, away from experiencing the delight of the greatest treasure there is: the experience of unconditional and unlimited joy. As human beings do not have access to that inner treasure, they are forever looking outside for worldly treasures that keep them in an unending circle of dissatisfaction. The light within contains it all. Through negative emotions, wrong believes, pain and fear, the inner light has been hidden and with it all it contains for us. Then Man has lived a lie: to think that the solution to his existence was in finding a paradise outside, and in creating a comfortable world that would provide him with all he has not found within him… and this has been his trap.

"Love is the power to attract all to you"

This is a move away from your vision of limitation towards a vision of totality and plentitude, manifesting in your life as your full potential. Then anything is possible. If the Violet Light was activated in everyone, everything would go much better at the individual level and in the world at large. Love is the power of the Universe: it is what makes things come about. Since that power is not fully awakened in people, it is no mystery why things work the way they do. If you want true changes, you need to face the facts that make them happen. You

5

want to open your heart since it contains all the treasures of life. Peace, power, love, healing, youth, beauty, prosperity, unity, freedom, joy come from an open heart. They don't come from anywhere else. The search after all things is the search after love, because it is love that brings everything to Man. But humanity has not realized that yet. The reality is very simple: God, the Source of all life, has all the power, wisdom and love that you need – that you will ever need. It is the absolute source of prosperity in all areas. The level in which you do not experience full prosperity in any area of your life, is the level of your disconnection from this Divine Power Source. You need to improve your relationship with It. This violet energy is a direct way to do it, and therefore a way to fully open the door to all that abundance. Why is light so important? It is the power of creation: the power of the Universe. Light is what creates. So if your inner light is active, you can have access to that power of creation. The Violet Light not only activates your inner light, it is an energy you can hold on to and use any time to create your true prosperity.

HOW LIGHT WORKS

In essence we are light. Although our light has fallen into a deep sleep, the original spark of light is still capable of being fully awakened. Everything is light. Light gives life. It becomes dense and turns into matter, so that it can manifest in the physical world. This is the only way there can be life here. Plants have the power to absorb sunlight and to create matter from it: crystallized light. Then plants give food to all. Animals, humans we all eat that crystallized sunlight. It is a lower version of the light, but it still contains its life giving essence. I remember seeing amazing stalactites of resin hanging from hollow pine trees. They looked like perfect reproductions of solidified, translucent rays of golden light, illumined by the sunlight. It was like light shinning on itself. Amber is just that: solidified sunlight. We are also crystallized light.

Light is power, intelligence, love of God. Through ignorance of the basic truths of life and how to live with them, human beings have become solidified as they moved away from the life-giving light, losing their power and love as they lost their luminous quality. Rigidity comes from lack of light and eventually this leads to senility and death. An injection of light brings anyone to life. Therefore this is the way to rejuvenate, to have energy and to make things work. The Violet Light breaks down rigidity and returns the luminous quality to all beings. Only in light is there life. Where there is no light, there is no life. The activation of the light within you, is the activation of your power, love and wisdom. This is the secret of life:

**"The more light in you, the more adaptable
and prosperous you are."**

The key lies in removing crystallizations, the blockages created in the absence of light. The Violet Light dissolves or shatters blockages, allowing light to enter again into all areas of you and of your life, producing an increase in your prosperity.

**"The key to prosperity is the amount of light
active and available."**

LOVE IS THE POWER YOU ARE LOOKING FOR

> *"The ego is trying to teach you
> how to gain the whole world and
> lose your own soul. The Holy Spirit
> teaches that you cannot lose your
> soul and there is no gain in the world."*
> – A Course in Miracles

The Violet Light is the return of the love power. This means that through the Violet Light all your love power is awakened; that creates a field of energy that attracts all the bounty of life to you. This powerful light has the power to restore the heart back to love. Love is the key because love is the greatest power and force there is. It is the power that Is. It is such a powerful vibration that there is nothing that has more light and power in the entire Universe. It is so powerful that the whole Universe is at its feet. If you truly love, the whole Universe will be at your feet, because the energy of the Universe, the particles of energy that create everything obey the power of love: it is their Master. Therefore you will manifest what you want through love. Those particles of energy will organize themselves to create what love commands. If you are "in love," they obey the love in you. This is the highest Metaphysics, the most sensible, the most accessible. Hence:

"If you want something, love it."

This is why love is the abundance people are looking for, because it is love that attracts everything to them. People are looking, and that search takes the form of objects and circumstances. If everyone realized that it is love they are looking for in those things, and that through love awakened inside they could get everything they look for, their lives and the planet would change radically. Humanity does not recognize this fact as yet, and thinks that what it needs is something else. People think they need things and events to be all right. Love is the only thing that will fulfill them truly. This is why, when there is no true love in people they become consumers of life: one thing after another. It is useless to try to fulfill a thirst with something else than what does the job. If one is thirsty of water, there is no point in insisting on food, or looking at pictures of water. Only the real thing will work.

"Man's search for fulfillment in the outside world has been, is, and will be doomed to failure, because it is the wrong search."

If love guides your life, everything will work. You put love in front and everything else will follow. Until love is not ruling your life, your life will not work correctly. The amount of love lacking in you is the measure of your unconsciousness, it portrays the level of unconsciousness ruling your life. As we become more conscious, we

8

become more loving too. The quantum leap waiting for humanity is a leap of love. A rising of our light, is a rising of our love.

The situations and beliefs people experience in their lives: life is stressful, fear and anxiety, loneliness and separation, lacks of any kind, arise because people do not have all the soul power available. So substitutes of this power have to be found. Activating the light power is the way to get rid of those unbalanced life conditions and the way to have peace, because then no human being will go to another for obtaining power because he has found it inside, and through that power he can manifest anything outside.

Human beings wrongly believe that others are their source of power. God is the supplier, but if they cast Him away, where are they going to get their power from? Man ignores Him and then pesters his fellow beings with demands for power. Then all interactions and relationships become power struggles. We must leave others alone. God is the source of supply. We have to live this truth. Then we will have relationships in harmony, because they will be ones of giving and sharing not of taking. Once people access all the power through their connection with God Source, all fights for power will be over.

LOVE MOTIVES

"Become free in love."

In life there are only two motives to act: love and fear. Most of the time people act out of fear. This comes from negative karmas. Those karmas have to be liberated and dissolved. In that transformation the motives for action based on fear, are changed for motives of love. It is necessary to increase the personal light to be able to choose. With the average level of light human beings have now, it is not possible to choose. As the light increases, people are able to choose peace instead of separation, love instead of fear, positive loving actions instead of selfish reactions of defense.

The more light is active in you, the more you are able to choose, you are at peace and your life works. But you need an agent that increases your light. The best agent is light itself. Within light, there is the Violet Light. It activates intensely your Inner Light. This is because from the spectrum of light, violet has the highest frequency of vibration. If we look at the rainbow, we see there are two colors at the ends: red and violet. Red is the lowest frequency and violet the highest. The rainbow colors are placed in ascending order of vibration. Although the violet light we deal with here is not the light of the rainbow, but rather a cosmic ray of light of unlimited reach, the principle is the same.

The amount of light you have active is easy to know. Just consider these points:
- If you act from love motives
- If you have a good amount of inner peace
- If most things in your life work
- If there is harmony in your personal environment
- If there is little or no suffering in you
- If you feel a great degree of completion

If any of these fails, your Inner Light is not strong. It needs to be awakened further. The Violet Light can help you with it. Then it is possible to choose love as the motive from which to act.

THE HIGHEST FREQUENCY OF LOVE

"The Violet Light is about putting
love of the highest frequency into your life."

The Violet Light is the love power of God at its highest. Here we have a love that is fully merged with the power of God. He offers this form of His Grace to bring to mankind a new type of love. Things don't take so much effort any more: things happen out of this love. It is so powerful, so deep, that we can know the sweetness of God and be

manipulative tendencies of our egos, so that we can allow love to manifest through us – thus becoming expressions of love. The hard work is asking yourself: "What is my mind doing?" at any time, to see how often it is coming, not from love or loving intent, but from selfish interest. This will place you in a position to be able to do something about it, and therefore it will allow you to transcend completely that tendency of the ego mind to want to be center of the Universe.

God is teaching us about Him in our way to understand what love is. Love is what we are, so we are learning about ourselves, about our true nature. This is a school of love – the Universe. In it, we learn to love as God loves.

"LOVE IS ALL THERE IS"

– CHAPTER 2 –

•

IMPORTANT CONSIDERATIONS

"The truth is, God is an
immense benevolent force."
– Kahan

GOD BEYOND INTERMEDIARIES

We have to finish with the madness that we are sinners. The original and only sin is to live separated from God, not because this is a sin but because it is self-destruction and therefore an act against life. In this state of affairs Man lives a life devoid of all real sense, caring only for himself and his possessions, including dear ones, without thinking about what was before birth and what would be after death. A life like this has no ultimate objective and therefore one can cheat any time. Generally, most people are nice to others – let's say kind to a point. But it does not go very far beyond social conventions. In the vision of society and therefore of the human mind, it is accepted that you can act without considering others at any given time, in your own self-interest. This is because there is no Dharma, which is right action illumined in love, consciousness and compassion: the law of Love, the law of God. Since the average relationship Man has with God is very poor, the relationship with that law of love is also very weak. Why do better? Who is watching? If we do not understand that Karma exists, why bother to do extra effort to be more loving, kinder, more selfless? The truth is – and this is perhaps the greatest lesson for Man to learn at this time – that no matter what, everything is an issue between you and God. This leaves everybody else out of the board that rules your life, because at that board only you and He seat. Which in practical terms means, it does not matter what happens outside, it

15

does not matter if somebody is watching or not, you act from the highest motive, you give your best regardless.

For a great amount of people in humanity life is about caring only for themselves, and about doing the necessary to live this way, although many times it appears very politically correct. Since they do not feel accountable to God or to a High Principle, it is as if God was not there. So to what law of an invisible God must they be loyal to? To what law of good loving behavior? You, as a human being, must have fidelity to a greater cause: to the light, to love, to an open heart, to the peace of God. If not you can easily be a victim of any idea, current manipulation, crazy behavior or even of your own obscure arguments. You can let yourself be carried away by any argument. So there is no hope for you in that. This is so when life is lived without association or loyalty to a greater principle.

On the other hand, true is that millions of people in the world worship God and are faithful to their idea of Him. Most probably you are one of them. They know the principle we call God is love and feel this is true deep inside. Therefore they try to live a life of love according to the feeling of their heart and to the principles of their religion. But God does not hide in temples. This is a distorted view of Him. If we do not know God away from temples, we won't live a life of love outside of them, and this is what happens to most of humanity.

It is my experience to have seen ordinary places being transformed into sacred spaces, where the presence of God could be felt. This is because people have meditated in them or a spiritual initiation has been given there. A hotel room has many times become a temple because of this. I have experienced it with mine and other spiritual events I have had the Grace to assist to. Yet religions at large have claimed to have sole ownership of the places where God dwells and of the "ways" to God, and then thought they had the right to divide people into the "faithful to God," who visit those institutions and the "unfaithful ones," who do not share those spaces with their associated practices. So mankind in this distorted view becomes a group of sinners, divided into the ones who become saved by following a specific religion, and the ones beyond hope. This is total manipulation. A distorted vision of things that has been ingrained in people's subconscious for many centuries, and from the moment of birth, with the resulting traumas that are one of the worst inheritances of our modern world.

If I have been able to bring to ordinary places a holy vibration, where a powerful sacred atmosphere could be felt and entered into in order to have a spiritual experience, and they were not temples or churches as we define them, it means I have done it out of my direct connection with the Divine. It is the divine power in Man, when expressed, that creates a temple and his way of life from there is a true religion. We have to recognize the true power given to Man through his purified heart, to access contact with Heaven. If God is seen as living inside every human being as His own temple, as it is in reality, God will be seen manifesting in everyone and anywhere, and the mere house of any man will be perceived as the temple of God.

The truth is there are spiritual planes. You, as an individual, can and should access these planes with your spiritual work and the right guidance. That is all. You do not need to depend on spiritual or religious systems. Have them and use them but don't depend on them. Obtain the support, the guidance the spiritual revelations from them, but do not loose perspective. It is not about joining a specific religion or another type of spiritual path, it is about God. The temple is the heart, there is where God dwells. Religion is what comes out of the heart: Love. Jesus did not say: "follow religion." He clearly taught to find God in the heart. Any man can access God in the heart, and any man should have the right to the divine guidance available from true sources to do it fully and to be told this truth. And then to experience it for himself. The true purpose of any path to God should be this. This is God oriented purpose. Any other purpose is Man purpose. But there is a lot of confusion about God and about following "His" ways, because a lot of the spiritual beliefs and practices in the world are related to guilt and judgment, and therefore they do not work as they should.

If a man sees himself as a sinner, he will see his brothers as sinners. If he judges himself because he does not feel pure in the eyes of God, he will judge others too. Does this sound familiar? So how can any man following a spiritual doctrine based on that find peace, love and God? The proof is in the state of the world: is it a loving world that manifests the true teachings of religions? Many people follow religions, not God. Many religious structures have created a false idea and vision of God, and many are also empty of true spiritual transmission: Grace transmission – the energy of The Holy Spirit. We cannot expect spiritual paths devoid of such divine energy, to be highly spiritual. They cannot be a very transforming influence. If there was true spiritual transmission – transmission of spiritual experience – in them, people would manifest a state of grace and light in daily life. This would show as true compassion and true strength; it would be reflected as tolerance, humility, love and wisdom. People's ability to change for the best, would be an obvious manifestation in them. Inner peace would be their general state of consciousness and service, their common practice. But although sometimes the most committed people to a religion do show those traits, the greater number of followers do not. Commitment to God and His cause opens the doors of Grace regardless of the name of your path.

The truth is, God is not dependent on religion. God Is. Religion was created as a way to access God. But the problem is that many religions have lost a lot of the sense of Truth, due to their own disconnection from the Divine. If there was truth in them, the world would be in another state. Where there is connection with the Divine, things work and that means peace, love and harmony. Truthful words may not contain Truth as a divine experience, if in the vehicle that transmits them, be a person or an institution, there is not a direct connection with the true inner experience of God, enabling it to channel His Grace.

People are not sinners, they are ignorant, confused and therefore mislead. If people were sinners, the power and light of God would not be in them. Either, they would have been taken away from people, or they would have never been given to them in the first place, and God has never done one or the other. We all have the divine gifts within us. But many do not know how to access them. We all have been told many lies about this fact, which if we have not torn apart yet will tear us apart eventually, especially through the belief that we are sinners, guilty of some sort of aberration and that we are powerless in redeeming ourselves. The only redemption necessary and the only one that works, is to turn to God. This is done by recognizing Him inside. Because there is no peace or freedom for any man, unless he turns within himself. Some spiritual paths and certain religions help with that a great deal, because they do have a true spiritual connection and their people are able to pull in the Grace of God. But their true mission should be to provide a divine connection for the individual, that he or she can develop to a point where the institution is not needed any more, because the individual has developed a direct relationship with God, becoming independent of the institution. He has received a transmission of Grace and from that moment, he can access it directly. Then he can go to spiritual activities to share, give and receive. And he should be a recognized bearer of the flame of God, who can speak on His behalf from his inner divine experience of Him.

But any spiritual system that pretends that only priest type figures are the ones who know, understand and are qualified to speak about God as His representatives, because they have studied religious matters, is partly a misleading system and as such it does not hold the highest truth. The individual who knows about God is the one who has had the experience of God. And the truth is that there are many out there who could enlighten masses out of their own spiritual experience of God, and have not stepped once into the seminary.

In turning to God, we stop feeding the belief of being sinners. This cannot be resolved in itself by purification, as inflicting pain in one way or another: not by punishing oneself. This does not clean anything. It is done just by turning to the light, embracing it and leaving aside all else, rejecting all that which is not light.

The ego is the devil. Within every man there is this unenlightened personality and consciousness, which is the one who acts with no love. Selfishness, pride, fear, anger, criticism, judgment, and many others alike are its qualities and allies. Within everyone also there is the light of God, the enlightened consciousness that expresses love, kindness, serenity, peacefulness, compassion, power and lives in unity. The sin is to live in the obscure personality, to believe that this is what we are, such abomination. To turn to God is to go to the place of light within, and to realize that this light is the presence of God in us. There is where we want to be because in it, there is peace. But Man has been divided in himself into these two entities. So there is separation within Man and therefore fight. The ego personality does not want to die, it wants to rule – and the God part within is sleeping. The way for every man is to awaken the God part inside and to illumine the other, because it is the one that creates hell in him and literally drives him there. As long as Man lives in the ego obscurity he is in the hands of the devil inside him. It is a kingdom of no love and unhappiness. God does not punish you for being there. He does not need to; that is hell itself: constant suffering. God wants you to know Him because that knowledge is your liberation, and also because He is the only place of light and peace for you. God knows that, but we don't. Therefore we often see God as "bad" because we believe He "wants" to take something away from us, and that He wants us to "buy" His ideas. The only thing God wants to take away from you is your ignorance. In this way you stop suffering and find everything He has already given you. But such love we do not know on this Earth and therefore we are suspicious of Him. We are so foolish. God is available through the heart. There is no sin other than forgetting God.

You are not a sinner you deserve it all.

TRUE PROSPERITY

True prosperity is the end result of this process. As we release the feeling of being in sin, the doors to abundance open for us. We don't stop the flow of universal bounty into us any more. Moving away from the limited idea of prosperity as "financial prosperity," we have to generate a new understanding of prosperity: True Prosperity. This means:

"Advancing in every area of life"

Which implies limitless abundance in whatever area – having the quality and the ability to prosper. In a word: moving forward, ahead and away from limits. Be it spiritual prosperity or material prosperity.

Prosperity = "Things go well"

We want to get rid of Karma and unconsciousness, so that the prosperity of the Universe flows into us and brings Grace, abundance and love to our lives. The Violet Light in releasing karmas, limits and negativity provides the vibration of prosperity according to the Divine Principle of unlimited abundance and evolution – which Man deserves as his divine right. Negative karma does not let you enter into abundance and prosperity. This karma is eliminated raising your vibration. High vibration produces prosperity and therefore abundance.

The extremely high spiritual vibration of the Violet Light, is what is missing in the human being to close his evolutional cycle and enter into the new era of light. It is a divine connection, an awakening to the divinity he is. This is the end of his search. In it mankind is put back in contact with the source of his inner prosperity. The Violet Light has the power to move all situations in the direction of true prosperity.

**"High vibration brings true prosperity;
it moves everything ahead."**

THE TYRANNY OF GUILT:
THE SOURCE OF SUFFERING

There is nowhere written in the Universe that you have to suffer. Maybe in books written by humans with a human mind. The only cause of suffering is absence of love. From it comes the feeling that you do not deserve love or joy because you are guilty. This takes many forms. Feeling guilty keeps in you the belief that you must be punished, that you do not deserve the joys of life. Guilt is not the solution to anything; it never gets liberated by itself and the solution it seeks is never found. I am not talking here of the guilt one feels when intentionally doing something wrong. But about the guilt that tells us we do not deserve happiness or joy, by the mere fact that we exist. The main accomplice of your suffering is yourself. Obviously this is so at the unconscious level. The unconscious feeling that you are guilty tells you, you do not deserve goodness. Because there is the belief in guilt in your mind, that belief ensures that you suffer, since it is in charge of creating situations that make you suffer. The tyranny of guilt is merciless, and it will take you as far as you let it.

The Universe is a benevolent place and God the most benevolent of all beings. We have been told the contrary. Everyone believes it and therefore the collective unconscious creates it all the time. You can wake up from this bad dream, if you want to, and realize that you deserve to be well, that you deserve a life without suffering. You are not guilty. You can allow the Violet Light to help you see without veils, so you get to appreciate this truth objectively for yourself.

Joy: The only truth

As you start believing in joy, your vision will change and you will see the true goodness of the Universe and the benevolence of God. You will understand that He has never wanted suffering for you. God gave Man free will to choose. The choices that led to suffering were Man's creations. But Man can also choose light and happiness. You can avoid anything you don't want by being present and being conscious: being conscious in the present. This implies consciousness and decision. But if your consciousness and decision power are weak, you need to make them strong, you need to recover them so you can avoid all you don't want. And one thing you surely don't want is the tyranny of guilt and the suffering it brings you.

We have also been told that God is love and that He is in Heaven. So Heaven must be the abode of love. This means that God supports love. Heaven must be what it is because there is no suffering in it. If God is the Lord of Heaven, He supports Heaven and therefore what makes Heaven be what it is: love and joy. Has God ever said to you that you must suffer? How could He if He is the Lord of Heaven, the place of love? So where did that believe about guilt and suffering come from? It is an inheritance of the human race. So it is a story told by humans, those beings that are not in Heaven and that do not really understand the ways of Heaven and of God. You are the sovereign of your life. You must take total responsibility for it. Create joy, do not expect it to come from somewhere else. If you wait for it you are assuming you are guilty and joy won't come to you; you are believing you don't deserve it. Assume from this moment on that you can create what you want because you deserve it. Do it sowing the right seeds. Do not accept fatalism; you will have it. Bad seeds create ill crops. So don't expect peace as a result of unloving actions. Change them for good loving actions and you will see how suffering disappears from your life. Then you will understand joy is the only reality.

Life responds to you the way you expect it will. So you are creating what happens. Try to make your decisions taking full responsibility for creating heaven for you and for others. It is about regaining control. And the decision to act in joy because you deserve it, is fully yours. Guilt takes away your joy and tells you, you do not deserve it. It takes away your power to act freely. You need to put yourself in a position of power in which every time, you have the choice to open the door to heaven and peace. And from that position you become able to make the best choice. It is a weak position the one in which you do not exercise your power to choose goodness. Maybe in the past humanity believed it had to suffer. Maybe it believed it was guilty as a natural condition. Now there is a choice. There is a lot of Grace available. You can use Grace like never before to solve things. To become free or happy, you don't have to suffer any more. You do not have to pay a price, it is your right to be happy. I mentioned this in the introduction. Try it long enough and you will see it for yourself. Precisely the power of Grace is redeeming. But let go of your suffering, of the need for suffering. Do not be attached to your suffering.

You have to be clear on one thing: in choosing joy you are safe. In choosing not to repeat self-destructive habits, you will be fine and safe. You just have to exercise that power in the present; don't delay it any longer. Act on this right now. If you feel guilty about being well, happy, prosperous, do not listen to it; it is a sign that there is no truth in that feeling. We need to develop the certainty that nothing will happen to us because of choosing the right self-enhancing actions in freedom from fear, supported by clear faith. Have the certainty that you will be safe. It is a matter of choosing freedom, of daring to be free even if others around us do not.

We can choose joy regardless of what institutions or unenlightened societies say, knowing we won't be punished for it. We must live understanding that; it is our divine right to do so. Seek joy. God is joy. Life is what you want it to be. The Universe is like a big screen, it projects the movie you want to see. And it does it out of your own script. If you don't want to see a scary movie, change your script. Dare to do it. You can.

•

GOD IS NOT AN OPTION

> *"Can any hide himself in secret*
> *places that I shall not see him?*
> *Do not I fill heaven and earth?"*
>
> — Jeremiah, 23:24

God is not an option, just as life is not an option. And if you are familiar with reincarnation you know that life doesn't end, and if you are not, you should know that the life essence of all beings goes on after what is called "death" – it cannot be stopped. We are so mistaken as humans thinking that we control things. Life is beyond us and greater than us. It happens as breathing happens and it is not in our control. Breathing is not an option. You cannot stop it. Life is beyond our will, we can only surrender to it. If God was an option, sooner or later the Universe would collapse. Surely someone somewhere would choose to depart from God, and since God is life he would certainly and truly die along that path. Then others too, would disintegrate away from life following that same path. Life cannot be separated from us and since God is life, God cannot be separated from us.

We all look for a place of safety and comfort, which we as humans have mostly looked for in the external world. But it has not been found. This is because that state of affairs does not exist in the external world. We all look for it nonetheless because deep in our soul, though unconsciously, we know there is something – a reality – that is permanent, unchangeable and totally reliable. We seek that because we know it is there. We are just looking for it in the wrong place and are forever disappointed. There has to be a reality that supports everything, a limit with which to function so that things don't fall out of Creation. There has to be a power such that when something goes wrong, it is saved again. We all know that deep inside. This power is what we call God. The place to find that elusive safety is in Him. It is obvious that there is a higher power, a Universal Intelligence, otherwise the Universe just wouldn't be what it is. A person that denies God – as that Universal Intelligence – is a scared person. So we need to understand what we do to avoid this reality: the issue of thinking God is an option.

Our ego minds think that they are in control, not wanting to see what is obvious: the body works, the heart functions, the sun comes out, plants grow and you and I do not have to get involved in any of that to see it happen. This is enough to shatter any thought system based on the belief, that ego mind power is the thing. So power is there acting, creating, making it all happen… and we think we have to sort it all out. It is done. There is a Universal Intelligence doing it. What we really want to know is how to plug into that main power and make it work for us. We want to know how to connect everything to it, because then it all gets an injection of life from the Source. Then it all develops, evolves, heals, expands, blossoms, excels. There is no real success – complete, thorough and sustainable – without connecting to God's power. The option given here for connecting to God's power is the Violet Light.

People think: "When I have that good job everything will be okay, will be financially secure…" and so on. They seek a career as the goal in life, to become something and then everything else can work from there. But it doesn't. Things go up and down, things change and power cuts… They are safety looking and they are pretty unsafe. The truth is that things won't be okay until you make God your career. That means knowing and understanding the power source that He is. Now, if you think this is for priests think again: God is the force that creates everything including you. So if you want to know the secrets – how everything works – you have to get to know Him. If you don't like the word God, call it "Universal Source." If you think: "I don't believe in God or in anything," remember what I said before about this. But if this is the way you want to look at it, that's fine. It means you believe in yourself, and discovering yourself is what this is all about. But you will have to acknowledge at some point in time, that there is a force or power out there that created you and others, the Earth and the Universe. If not, you are going to have a really hard time explaining coherently to yourself how the Universe, life and you came about.

That force of life pulsates in you and getting to know it, is getting to know the truth of yourself. You might not like to accept a power in you, you don't know fully but here is the limit: you just have to come to terms with it. So whether you accept it as God or as a Universal Source, or whether you deny it, it does not make a difference on how things are, that force exists and it is out there and in everyone. The tree might say: "I don't care much for the roots," but it doesn't matter if the tree doesn't care for them, of if it doesn't like them, or if it doesn't know they are there, the roots are still supporting its life. God is the same for us.

I have explored and investigated life by means of many spiritual currents, and through them I have found and touched a powerful force behind everything. As I delved deeply into the experiences I encountered, I have been increasingly blessed in myself and in my life. The door to the power source of God in me has been opened, and I can tell you that if people knew the blessings, the ecstasy and the freedom that are inside of them through that door, they would all dive into it this very second. Until you make God – that Source – "your career," your aim in life, things won't work properly for you. Be sure of that. And I don't mean just working, I mean everything surpassing your wildest dreams.

All life is there set for you to know yourself, to know God in you. Life is not about becoming a successful lawyer or a great artist, it is about knowing what life is about and what you are about. Then becoming a lawyer or an artist will be your way of living it, and it will certainly be a lot easier, besides you will be much more successful. The ego mind wants to think it has power, therefore it conveniently omits the reality of how things are in order to believe that it is safe because it controls, and that as far as it is in control things are fine. This is a dangerous place to be because they are not. The mind uses the power God gives it to deny God. It is truly amazing. Just observing the daily miracles I have mentioned above, would be enough to bring anyone to humility. Power beyond us is there. We just have to open our eyes to see it. So I recommend this as an exercise to you: to seek, to see and to watch that power every day in your life, and then observe what life would be like without it. That power gives life to all life in so many ways.

Traveling through different regions of the Earth, I have been amazed at the spectacle Nature offers. I have seen lizards running down rock walls at great speed, cats and squirrels going up trees like there is no gravity. I have seen deer jumping great distances over the ground, humming birds doing anything in the air... then I observe human beings and see them so slow, heavy, bound to gravity. But the human being has the greatest power: the ability to know God. He can do this through self-consciousness. This is the greatest gift given with the human form. It should be fully used.

The doors for connecting to that Universal Power Source are open. The difference of being in contact with it, is like the difference between using a bulb to light your life or using the light of the sun. You cannot make God an option because if you do, you end up living a mediocre life, maybe not in your terms but in the terms of Universal Intelligence, your Christmas presents are still wrapped.

As with the roots of the tree, we do not have an option: all life power is there for us. If we prefer to think we do not have roots and in them a power that supports and sustains us, we might be missing the best thing in life and with it, the treasure it brings: the source of all bounty.

God is not an option and this is really a blessing.

PART II

GETTING READY
FOR THE JOURNEY

"The ego will never see truth.

Truth is the only thing

the Divine Self sees."

– K a h a n

– CHAPTER 3 –

•

THE RINGING OF THE BELLS:
GETTING THE LUGGAGE READY

"We need to have a humble recognition of where we are, to acquire the eyes to see the path to follow out of our ignorance."
– Kahan

We are in changing times. As many books and messages are saying we are in the final times of the paradigm that has lived on the Earth for thousands of years. But the many seers that predicted the end of the world for these times, forgot to add the most important part of the sentence, "…as we know it." So these are the final times or the end of the world as we know it because the world changes, it does not disappear. It is the end of the play, so the stage changes. When a play is over, the team in charge takes down the stage. They dismantle it and put up another one for the new play. This is the same. The play we've had on the planet is over, so everything is being dismantled – within and without – to manifest a different play on a different stage.

This change is the evolutional quantum leap of humanity in which we are all immersed. In cosmic evolution when a cycle comes near its closing point, it starts going up thus creating a spiral. To make the trajectory of the circle move up so that it does not end up as a circle, and therefore where it started, extra energy is necessary. An input of new energy has to thrust the closing circle up, to create the upward moving spiral. It is like a jumping board that gathers momentum before the jump. That input of extra upward energy at this cosmic planetary time, is the Violet Light. This energy increases the vibration

31

of the whole Earth system making it go up, to reach the point of the spiral. This is absolutely essential. The Violet Light creates a spiritual revolution which includes letting go – forgiving – the old, the past and then, light in weight, we can rise to higher spheres of consciousness: love and wisdom. In this process karmas have to be dissolved like blocks of ice, which melt in contact with the intense spiritual heat provided by the high spiritual energy of the Violet Light.

So we find ourselves in the middle of the ringing of the end bells. This time they are not the bells of the New Year, but the bells of the New Era. It has some particulars to it. The most important one is that we must be ready. This means that we have to prepare our luggage, but a very special kind: we have to prepare the heart. How? By opening it truly. You can only take with you on this journey love, forgiveness, truth. And hence we have a humanity going crazy because the bells are ringing and it does not have the luggage ready. Too many fears are still there, resentments, anger, aggression, intolerance, masks, deceit, pain and all that cannot go into the luggage. So the time closes in and we are not ready for the leap. That's why everybody is in a kind of deep personal crisis, in an attempt to solve everything that is not coming from loving intent, once and for all. Preparing the luggage is about getting rid of the excess weight. Whether you know it or not, you and all are getting ready for that moment, getting rid of karmas and the past at a great speed. This is what originates the apparent global crisis and the feeling that there is "no time."

Humanity at large is not manifesting love, and the place where we go – the higher planes of vibration – cannot be entered with anything else. We cannot enter with such low frequencies as fear, resentment and selfishness. All those have to be processed, integrated or transmuted. This is what the Violet Light offers: a global and extremely fast release of karmas and negativity, low-vibration energies and realities, in a word obscurity, at an individual and global level.

There is not much cosmic time left for the access of the Earth to a higher dimension of consciousness. At that time, everyone upon the planet must be vibrating in a higher frequency. Given the urgency of this "ascension," a powerful energy is needed capable of accelerating the vibration of the planetary system in a very short time. That energy is "The Seventh Ray" or The Violet Ray of light, which has the highest vibration of all the available rays of light. It is thanks to this process that the human being will manifest the divine qualities of his being: love, peace and light.

DESTINATION OF LIGHT: AQUARIUS

"Life is the evolutionary opportunity to acquire your highest consciousness."

The destination point has been called: "The Age of Aquarius." Aquarius as destination means a change of vibration, change of consciousness, change of paradigm: a change of structures. We are witnessing the fall of all planetary structures: mental, emotional, physical, religious, educational, political, social, economic structures. All the structures are now being shaken and they are falling, so that new ones can be built based on truth, harmony and light: a new consciousness.

Separated from the Divine Will through our own human choice, we have created the perfect cocktail for a world without love: a humanity unbalanced, disharmonious and confused. We cannot negotiate further with time and with Karma. We are in times of facing the truth. So if you are not living your highest truth, you will live the consequences. The time has come for all to become updated in all that is pending: repressed emotions, hidden feelings, life plans, issues not forgiven in order to enter into peace. A time to know who we are in reality, a time to reconcile with everything that is not integrated in us, and with all that we have not actualized in ourselves. Then taking hold of the new frequencies, we can reach the destiny of light. This is for everyone. There is no option.

DANCING TO A NEW RHYTHM

"The acceleration of things is forcing us to drop the mind and face the present with the heart."

The frequencies of the planet are changing. We have gone from dancing a slow waltz, to trying to keep up with a fast rock and roll. So we are learning the steps and the new fast moves to keep up with the new music. The reality is that we cannot enter into the Age of Aquarius if there is not a change in vibration. The present acceleration of life upon the Earth is produced by the Light of Aquarius, which is the Violet Light: the energy that manifests the qualities of Aquarius. A new era always comes with a new energy. As the new energy enters the planet, it changes the vibration of people changing their consciousness. Then the new era manifests itself from that new consciousness through people, in the structures of life and society.

As we are experiencing now, all the processes are being accelerated. Time itself seems to have become faster than ever before. Everything seems to be going at great speed: the processes we go through at work, in our relationships, even our own mental and emotional processes. It is as if someone had turned the accelerator to full speed. So we are finding we have to live with this new speed in everything we do. We have to learn to adjust to this new way of living life and relating to time. When I was touching this situation in my life a while back, I had to learn to deal with things in this new context as if I was learning again, for the first time, how to deal with life and time. It took me work, changes inside myself and in my life. But the most important lesson I learnt from it, was to set priorities in a new way. I started teaching what I was learning, whenever I approached an audience. The main thing was to ask them what they would do if they suddenly had less time available in the day. We shared the only sensible possible answer: drop things, set priorities. I summarized it this way: you focus on the important. This means that if we have gone from dancing to a slow rhythm to a fast one, the tempo is faster so we have to move faster to go along with it. Which means we cannot afford any more to look at the view because we have to get the work done, right here right now.

There are no delays. Now the moment you relax too much a pile of things appears before you, for you to sort out. And that pile might be of dirty laundry, pending issues at work or unsolved relationship problems. It might even be of personal projects you had in mind. The key to this situation is to face the present with the heart. This is the coded message. A message of engaging the heart in the here and now, for this is the way to get along with life in this new state of affairs we all upon the Earth are going through. Dealing with things with the mind, only causes delays in a time that requires immediate action from the right place, the place of truth, the place of love: the heart. If we are not capable of facing this way of acting, this will be our learning process. Operating away from the present or outside the heart, we will only run into trouble: piles and piles of things that burden us, as they confront us with our inability to connect with ourselves, and therefore with life and people from a direct, truthful and kind approach. We are learning to set priorities and to accept there are things we just have to let go. A great learning in detachment and flowing. There is nothing more immediate than the truth of the heart. There is nothing more real than the present. The mind needs time for its processes. The heart lives in the present, where there is no time. From it things do not accumulate. So the times are forcing us to move from operating from the mind, to operating from the heart. This is the only way we will find happiness.

The cosmic band that is playing this music at this new rhythm, is the "cosmic band of the Violet Light." This "new music" produces an acceleration in the evolution of human consciousness and that which before took many years or many lives to be accomplished, can now be done in just a few years or in one lifetime. This means that all who enter into contact with the Violet Light enter into a strong rise in vibration. This inevitably produces a…

DIVINE CONNECTION

A rise in vibration of this kind supposes the acceleration of the evolutional process of every person, towards his or her direct divine connection. This manifests in you as the awakening to the reality of God, being true and available to you. As the inner light seed inside everyone is stimulated by Divine Grace, there is a birth of the Christ Self or Divine Self. We are witnessing an expansion of the personal light in the whole of humanity, as a consequence of the manifestation of that Divine Self. A new dimension of inner peace and a direct communion with God, become available away from intermediaries, dogmas and conditions. It is in the re-connection with God that you acquire true power and love. The role of the Violet Light in this process is to speed up this re-connection, and as we see next, to return the spiritual sovereignty to the individual.

SPIRITUAL INDEPENDENCE

The Violet Light is God's Grace. This Grace is here to provide a liberation of the individual soul, not only from karmas and limitations, but also from belief systems, spiritual structures and dependency on spiritual figures. It is moving humanity towards the consciousness that the spiritual Master is inside, the temple is your body and the God you seek is your Higher Self. This realization is the only way to grant an individual with spiritual independence. True spiritual paths and their spiritual leaders have been very important, for they are the ones that in a long era of darkness and chaos, have held the high frequencies of spirit and brought light and a path to it to the world. But in a new world where consciousness and light are every day more available to everyone, such figures will take a new role: they will be the helpers and leaders to birth the new era of light and love upon the planet. It is right that they are, since they are more advanced, but not to create dependency. Their role will be to help people realize their own mastery, to help them become their own

Masters, in a way in which the individual will be spiritually empowered. Many are already doing it, and their great work will be shown as they help others reach the spiritual awareness they have themselves attained. As it was portrayed earlier on, once people's spiritual connection is strong through work and Grace, they don't need to depend on anyone. They can receive guidance at times, share spiritual revelations, learn from a Spiritual Master or other companions, but from the consciousness that they are independent. Direct communion with God is where the knowledge and the power to lead life comes from.

This independence is an advance state of grace and discernment, in which your own mastery is sufficiently awakened to identify your negative ego traps, and to have enough spiritual strength in order to channel God intent, not ego intent, so you are able to discern which one is which. Or else you cannot talk of spiritual independence. My work here is to bring the Grace of the Violet Light to you, so that you become spiritually independent – independent even of myself, through your direct connection with Grace and through your own effort. The aim is that you become the teachings themselves and turn into your own Master, as your inner light is activated inside and your soul love power manifested. The Violet Light will provide, stimulate or enhance your own direct connection with God Source. This is the way we are supposed to go. We are not meant to be forever dependent, we are meant to be spiritually independent.

"The Violet Light is spiritual wealth;
The Violet Light is Spiritual Royalty."
– Ericka Huggins

37

– CHAPTER 4 –

•

YOUR COMPANIONS ON THE JOURNEY

*"Wisdom and knowledge,
understanding and love,
come from being exposed
to higher energies."*
– Kahan

ENERGY MATTERS

Everything is energy. A table, a house, a human body... thought is energy. All energy vibrates. The difference between what one energy system looks like and another, is the pattern that created them and their rate of vibration. We will develop this later on to all its detail. Now we will look at the generalities of it. The two extremes in energy manifestation are matter and spirit. That which we call matter, is the densest and it is solid. The lighter one, spirit, is pure energy. Matter has low energy: it vibrates very slowly. That is why it is dense and opaque – with no light. Spirit vibrates very high, it is translucent. This is what spirit is: luminous – a very high energy of light. As energy vibrates higher, it has more light and therefore more consciousness. So it gets nearer to being spiritual, nearer to what we call God.

If we could increase the energy – the vibration – of a log of wood sufficiently, it would become light. As the vibration of energy of things increases, they start to acquire more light. This is the same with human beings, as their energy and vibration increases they radiate more light. Then they manifest more consciousness. Since the Violet Light is the highest vibration of energy, it can alter any energy state. Any other energy state has a lower vibration than the Violet Light, so you can positively affect anything in your life with the Violet Light. Therefore with this light you can influence emotional states, physical blockages, relationships, work circumstances, or any other events, including the increase of your soul's vibration, to access spiritual states towards your self-realization.

The Violet Light acts as an agent of change, because any vibration in touch with it, is altered and taken to a higher state of energy, increasing its light and therefore its consciousness. It is similar to when you put something cold next to a source of heat, that thing warms up. When something is heated in an intense fire, like wood, its energy increases so much that it radiates heat and light.

What is most relevant here, is to understand that any situation in life that is not working for you, has low energy. Relationship problems, financial difficulties, depression, unhappiness, anxiety, illness, fear, doubts, lack, absence of peace, sadness, are all states of negative or low energy. The positive states of prosperity, abundance, inner peace, health, harmony, empowerment, love, harmonious relationships, are all states of high energy – high vibration. So since anything can be changed because its energy can be affected, by applying high energy to mental negative states, for instance, you can transform them into positive, prosperous states.

ALCHEMY

Traditional alchemy looked at transforming lead or base metals, into gold. Base metals are dense metals because they have low vibration. Gold is the metal with the highest vibration. So alchemy is about raising vibration. Alchemy is not only about material things, it is also a process applied to human beings to take them from a basic or low state of vibration, and therefore consciousness, to the highest vibration: a high spiritual state. This would be the golden state for a human being. This is true alchemy, spiritual alchemy or inner alchemy the one that takes you to your "Christ Self" or "I Am" consciousness, your Higher Self. The power of the Violet Light is exactly this: the alchemical ability to transform you into your spiritual gold.

The name we can best give it is...

GRACE

> *"By Grace I live. By Grace I am released.*
> *Grace is acceptance of the love of God*
> *within a world of seemingly hate and fear.*
> *By Grace alone the hate and fear are gone."*
> – A Course in Miracles

"What is Grace?"
I ask the audience in my conferences. The best answer I was ever given was: "A Gift."

Grace is divine intervention. A true gift: liberating energy of love that comes from God. It redeems us. It liberates us. As human beings we have, at large, forgotten God and His Grace. We believe power only comes from us, from the ego, and we see the world we have. Why is Grace so important? Because it works; because it is divine intervention. That's why it works. But... what do I need Divine Grace for, especially if everything is going "so well" without it? Anybody ever thought there was a need for anything like that? "I never did," you might say.

Here is the truth. You need it:

- To transcend your limits.
- Because without Grace you are incomplete.
- Because it is natural. You were never supposed to do it all alone.
- It is the support of God.

- Without Grace you only have the power of ego and it is very, very limited.
- Without Grace you are not free, you have karmas to work out.
- With Grace and your effort you can go very far and become free.

You, as a human being, can transmute yourself alone – or with the help of your psychoanalyst. But you can only reach a certain point with your mind. What is God there for? Have we forgotten Him? He is our Father and Creator. Wouldn't He have a solution for the madness in which we are immersed as human beings? A solution to take us back to our divine state of peace, love and wisdom? A way to become one with Him again?

Of course He has. It is called Grace.

And as you open up to it, you find that it all works like never before. Now, we have it available in the form of a beautiful light of violet color. We have forgotten for too long our best ally and have changed it for a tricky one: the ego. With God, the Source, you have everything: total and perfect abundance of all. And I am not talking about material abundance, although that as well. We have said no to God with all He has for a sense of limited power and limits we call ego, just for the sake of self-importance.

"In God there is Grace. In the ego, disgrace."

Think about it. You may pray, you may believe in God, but have you accessed all the power in Him? How much do you still hold back and therefore depend on your ego power? More of this in the section: "The truth about surrender."

You need a partner, the best one. Because alone we have already seen the mess human beings can create. Jesus said: "I of my own self can do nothing," recognizing the need for the Divine Father and His intervention in all affairs. That was, and is, the attitude of a mighty spiritual figure. What about the attitude of the average man on the street? Or yours or mine? A matter for reflection.

Life is a tricky business full of uncertainties and limits. It is like a labyrinth and you only have half a map of it: the vision of your predecessors. And to make matters worse a broken compass that only works half the time: your repressed inner voice – inner compass or intuition. With that and your best wit, you try to make the most of it succeeding some of the time, failing the rest of it, but almost never able to get everything right at the same time. You walk this way, then the other in the labyrinth of life, but it really is your mind which is very much like a labyrinth.

One day... someone flying a helicopter stops right above you in the labyrinth. He yells:
"Hey, jump in and take a look at it from here."
He drops the ladder and you go up. Once in the helicopter you look down and say in relief:
"Now I understand it all!"
The pilot is busy. So he says to you:
"Okay, I have to go. Do you want to stay or do you want to go back?"
You obviously say without hesitation, in a humble tone – that is asking for mercy:
"I'll stay" ...and you are allowed to stay.

That's Grace.

UNDERSTANDING KARMA

You have all heard at some point about Karma. A lot has been said about it, and many concepts fly in our heads when we hear the word. But let's take a new vision at the old subject.

Karma is the distance that keeps you separated from God. God here will be your state of divinity. That distance is in reality how far away you are from knowing, experiencing and living fully that reality: "I Am Divine," since the inner spiritual self and God are one. You have to narrow that distance because while it exists, you are not living your true reality: your divine identity. Events, situations, people come up in our lives to help us narrow that distance, bringing us greater consciousness. Those events are "karmatic." They are often difficult as they imply facing up to our limits in all respects. Limits to love, to greater tolerance, to having faith, to being humble, to becoming compassionate, to developing our wisdom, our power, showing us our own distorted view of life: our own neurosis. In one word, those events are there to help us become greater human beings, so great eventually, that we become divine beings. We are already divine, we only have to realize it. The situations we encounter will take us nearer to realizing that, getting nearer to loving as God loves: unconditionally. So our limits are really limits to love itself.

If one is not in total identification with his divine consciousness, there is Karma. While there is identification with the ego consciousness as what we are – as our identity – there is separation and therefore Karma. Within Karma we can say there is "good karma" and "bad karma." Good karma might be that we, without much effort, become successful and wealthy in life. It is close to the idea of "good luck." Bad karma would be that no matter how hard you try, you cannot find a right partner and marry, for instance. I say this at the risk of over simplifying – because that situation in itself can be proven to be "good karma." "Bad karma" would be the karma that limits us, the one we want to get rid of. The greatest lessons almost always lie in it. Loneliness, financial difficulties, pain, suffering, illness... the list is endless. In reality, there is no such a thing as "good" or "bad" karma. Everything is Karma and we want to live a life so in tune with our divinity, that we generate no Karma. That, in the spiritual traditions of most of Asia is called a life in "Dharma" – that which is correct according to the law of God.

Karma is like a magnet. This magnet has a specific coding that attracts a situation to you. And it does it persistently. Anything recurrent that tends to repeat itself two or more times in your life, has the signature of Karma. You ought to start thinking that such situation is Karma and should start looking for a real solution to it. If it is a "difficult" karma, for instance: "all partners I attract are controlling and manipulative," this can really be a problem. And you try and there is no way to change that. Another example: every time a person gets a job, after three or four months something happens and he is out of work. The situations described above are not coincidences, they are there to teach you something. That something is to become conscious of the magnet you carry with you, and the coding it has, which undoubtedly is an area in your life where you are cut off from the Divine Source and thus, are separated from Its flowing Grace and abundance. In learning that lesson, the coding is deactivated and the flow of Grace and divine abundance is restored for you. Learning the lesson can be tricky, sometimes elusive; often not at all obvious to you. Sometimes you think you have learnt it, to find out that it still happens. The whole subject is quite mysterious and complicated, as you certainly know from your own experience. What do you do? Seek help. This is my work.

Imagine you have the karma "yyy," this is its code. It is placed somewhere in your energy system: chakras, aura, energy channels… wherever. This active magnet will attract to you the situation "yyy" from the world around you. If "yyy" means for someone: "I want to get closer to people and I end up alone," it means this is what she will attract to her and to her experience of life. The solution given in this book is: get connected with the Violet Light and use it. This light has the power to find that magnet and dismantle its power and coding, making it disappear from you. How? By the alchemical power of transmutation, which we will talk about in detail soon. We call it "transmute your karma" or "burn your karma." This means that the Violet Light can set you free. That's why with it, you can create your destiny: you are not forced any more to live and experience life dictated by the tyranny of Karma. As you acquire the power to burn your karma, you accelerate tremendously your spiritual evolution, as you gain the freedom to operate with more decision, power and love in your life. Later on, I will explain the techniques you can use. And before that, we will go through an activation that will connect you with the power of the Violet Light.

The Violet Light is a peculiar combination of two forces: the Blue Ray of Light and the Pink Ray of Light. If you like to play with colors or are a painter, you know the result of mixing blue and pink. You get exactly violet. As it happens the Blue Ray is the energy of the Will of God – the Power of God, and the Pink Ray is the energy of the Love of God. So both together = Love power. Can you think of anything more powerful than the Power and the Love of God together?

I can't.

PART III

YOUR JOURNEY TO FREEDOM:

THE COURSE OF
THE VIOLET LIGHT

"Every time you do not trust God
enough, your faith becomes weak.
Every time you renounce God,
you bring up an idol to compensate
for that lack of trust.
An idol will eventually fall.
God is inside. This is your Mastery.
Your devotion is to God, not to
something else. Not to fear, illusions,
ghosts, idols. Only to God.
This is your freedom."

— K a h a n

– CHAPTER 5 –

•

THE FOUNDATIONS OF THE WORK

"And ye shall seek me,
and find me, when ye shall
search for me with all thy heart."
– Jeremiah, 29:13

THE FACTS

- The Violet Light is an energy that comes from the highest spiritual planes. Therefore it is a spiritual path – meaning a path that takes you to spirit – to the true reality that you are.

- It has always been related to great Masters or Saints like Jesus, Saint Germain and others.

- It is very important now for the transmutation and liberation of anything, individual or Global, which is not harmonious, loving or perfect. Call it Karma.

- It is fundamental in order to accelerate our evolution and the planet's evolution, to bring us back to a global state of love, peace, and light.

THE OBJECTIVES

The objectives of knowing and working with this energy are that:

- You receive the activation – the permanent connection with the Violet Light.

- You understand how it works and learn the techniques to be able to use this energy properly.

- You raise your state of consciousness to peace, compassion and service.

- You transmute everything that is not peace, love and wisdom in yourself and in your life.

- You are active with this energy for your good and the good of others.

- You help your evolution and the evolution of Humanity.

- You help in the transmutation and elevation of the planet.

●

INVOCATION

This is a "read and do" book. Before we continue, you should do this invocation. It is the one used in the courses and it is very powerful. It will set up the energies for your experience and this will make the book not just a book you read, but a book you live. You are not alone. The Masters of Light are with you. I am with you.

Sit in a cozy comfortable place in your home. If you have a place where you meditate or pray, that's the place. Lower the light. Light a candle. Incense will help create the atmosphere. Nothing is a must, only your heart's desire to connect.

•

Start

Do not rush. Read and feel. Then read the next instruction.

Breathe deeply three times. Concentrate on the heart. Let go all barriers, all obstacles, all judgments. Let go all your ideas about yourself and enter the sacred space of your heart. Open your hands, palms up facing heaven.

Read this starting invocation aloud:

"I invoke the Violet Light, the Ascended Masters of Light, the presence of my Higher Self and the presence of God Divine Source, to be here with me now so that I am taken to the connection with the Violet Light through this work. Thank you."
Amen.

Continue with this:

"I ask that all the consciousness of this encounter and the Activation and Grace of the Violet Light, reach every human being, every sentient being and the planet. Thank you."
Amen.

Close your eyes and stay with the energy for a few minutes.

Without leaving your connection follow with this contemplation.

•

Practice

Heart Connection

You do not need to speak aloud here.

Close your eyes and ask yourself:

"In which moment of my life am I?"

"What is my being asking of me?"

"How do I feel?"

"Am I happy? At peace? Angry?

Tense? Worried? Disconnected?"

Listen to the answers that come from within. Take your time.
Look at them sincerely. Recognize the feeling, let it touch you. Don't reject it or deny it if it is unpleasant. Allow it to happen. Give it the space it needs inside you.

Listen to your Self for a few minutes.

In this state we ask for the Grace

Speak aloud with serenity and from the heart:

"I open up to life, to the Light to receive all that which I need, that consciousness, that clarity, those blessings – the Grace. I ask God, the Supreme Light that inhabits in my true being – the consciousness of my Inner Self – that He illumines me from within so that I reach total unity with my own being, my own Divinity and I attain inner peace, inner love. I ask for the Grace to be able to open up totally to the Violet Light to receive all its blessings. Thank you."
Amen.

Close your eyes and feel this experience in silence. Allow yourself time to stay in this state and when ready, come out of the contemplation giving thanks.

– CHAPTER 6 –

•

THE STATE OF AFFAIRS

*"When the ego gets in, it wants
to use it all for its purposes. When
God is there, He uses it all for love."*
– Kahan

At the beginning of the Violet Light courses I always ask the participants:

"What is the most critical problem of Humanity?"

The list goes something like this: fear; disharmony; lack of love; anger; ignorance; hatred; violence; anxiety; desire; frustration; agitation; separation…

Although all these are true, they all come from one thing: "The false sense of identity." All the answers on the list come from this. The false sense of identity, takes us to separation because we think as human beings that we are "this:" our body and mind. So we see our identity limited to our ego. In this false identity, bringer of separation, is where we have the origin of war, conflicts, racism and judgments like "they are the bad ones" and similar ones.

Why is this so?

If you see yourself as this limited ego identity, something or someone outside you presents an opposition to you by his mere presence. This means for your limited ego identity, that you have to protect and defend yourself because you can feel threatened by that presence: you have to "survive" – your defenses go up. This is how the false sense of identity operates at the base. The workings of this are often happening deep within the mind, at the subconscious level. The conscious external manifestation of this is distrust, suspicion, distance.

If you have the awareness that you and the other are "one" – the true sense of identity – where is the threat? There is none. There is no conflict; you don't feel full of fear and therefore having to defend yourself, because there is no one outside you that threatens you with his or her presence. There is nothing outside. If you are one with others you are big and not small, therefore you don't have to defend yourself. The result of this is peace.

In that state, you don't have to fight to assert yourself in the world in order to survive in your ego false identity. In any case, do you know who the other is? The other is you with another face. That's why Jesus himself said to recognize ourselves in the other's eyes. See yourself in them, in their smile, in their heart. Love them, you have nothing else to do, you have no other real, sane option. This is what you realize when you are in the "I Am Presence," the presence of your Higher Self.

But what happens with this false sense of identity? We think we are the ego: body, personality, mind. We think all these are "me," which is limited and therefore we have in it limited power. Because we think we are this ego, we believe power comes from it. Therefore the ego takes ownership of this power and seeks to increase it. The issue is that the ego does so through the ways of the ego: dominance, influence, violence, control, manipulation, no love and so on. So the ego plays at pretending it is God as it seeks to increase its power. The fact is that we are already God in essence, but we have not realized this at large.

True power is in spiritually awakened consciousness, that which is beyond the ego. It is in the "Self" who really is God inside, the Divine "I." If we recognize this fact we don't have to take power away from others to feed our own. And therefore we will be able to let go of the false identity and will unite ourselves with the true one. This way we become free. We don't need to associate with the ego identity any more. At that moment we free ourselves from the tendency of the ego to accumulate power, and from the belief that it is its own. Then the greatest thing occurs:

We free ourselves from all selfishness.

Great spiritual Masters have explained from their high state of consciousness, that due to our identification with the ego we keep in the wheel of birth and death: reincarnation. In it people go on dying and taking birth again and again seeking to get another body, another ego, simply because they believe that's what they are.

YOUR ENEMIES: THE MIND AND THE EGO

Here we are talking about the negative ego and the unenlightened mind. Your mind has a life of its own. Remember unsettling events in your life. What was your mind doing? during the day, and at night, could you sleep? And when there are no unsettling events, what is your mind doing? Can you stop its non-stopping madness?

The thing with the mind is that it says: "I know," "I can," "I control," "there is no problem." But this comes from a rigid, self-righteous, dominant attitude, where nothing or nobody is needed. The "all powerful" mind is the queen... until a wave comes. A huge wave comes into your life and shakes you right through. It hits you hard, and knocks you down. Does this sound familiar? But when the effect of the blow becomes weaker, the mind becomes strong again and says: "How, if I am in control? There is nothing outside my control. Ah! It was only a scratch. Here is my invincible, invulnerable image." The next wave is around the corner and after that one, many more even bigger. Then the mind does not get up... for a long while. What happens then is that humility starts to be born, the humility of the heart: the acknowledgement that God, that Universal Force, has the power, not the ego or the mind. Deep down they are doing us a favor.

One then weeps and the tears purify the wounds and purify one's pride, the pride of the mind that pretends to be all mighty and denies love, compassion, and the tenderness of the heart. Because it has taken on a throne that is not its own, a throne that belongs to the heart, because the kingdom of life is the kingdom of love. You can reach God through your heart, not through your mind.

Those tears mean that one has not been in touch with his feelings and with his heart for a long time. The mask is shattered, the shell we live in, with which we cover our heart and that it pretends to hide how nice we are. We are loving beings, vulnerable, tender, lovable... but not weak. It is a false conception that tenderness and goodness are weakness. The capacity to be oneself and to show how one truly is, is a strength many would envy. The mask is false, how can there be strength in it? "The hard," says Lao Tsu, "is friend of death. The soft and tender is friend of life."

Look at a baby. His power is awesome: everyone is tending to him. He is all vulnerable. He is the center of attention: the power of tenderness. He has everybody at his feet through it. It is such a real thing. We spend our lives trying to pretend we are something we are not, something we will never be, something that does not exist: superman or superwoman. We do it to get attention and love from others and end up alone. We are doing it wrong. Next time you want someone to fall in love with you, be vulnerable; it is irresistible.

To recognize our vulnerability is a total act of letting the ego go, and of trusting our vulnerable selves; an act of committing ourselves to live from there. This is true strength. The rigidity of the mask is sure death, in a relationship or in any aspect of life. It brings death because it is weakness. Trees bend and survive strong winds. The river flows beyond the rigidity of the rock. The water does not stop at the rock, the apparent obstacle. We humans do. Then we need psychotherapy because we stopped flowing at some point. Stopping is death, flowing is life. But try to destroy water... it is stronger than the rocks it erodes.

THE ONLY WAY: LOVE AND COMPASSION

"The Universe is about compassion.
If you are not in it, you suffer."
– Kahan

The issue in life is love and compassion. If you have not realized this, it is because you are still too absorbed with your small desires: the search for the satisfaction of your own selfishness. This is what keeps you unhappy. Giving yourself to life, seeking to give your best to others, looking for the greatest good for the greatest number, only then you move away from selfishness and you find true peace and happiness. This implies giving from love and being detached from any form of gain in it. If there is no detachment, there is self-interest in the action and you are giving because you want something in return. This giving is selfish. You must live the premise:

"I don't give to see what I get, I give for the sake of giving."

Compassion has to become a way of being, rather than a way you act in certain circumstances. To do this you must always be tuned in to life and to others, keeping the heart open. This means one great truth for all: "I am not the most important one." The Buddhists know this very well. Their highest teaching is to live a life of "Boddhichitta:" a life of Compassion. This way of life through compassion gives us a state of peace, an inner fulfillment. In this way, your experience of life is totally different and the world becomes a place of harmony and love, a place in which everybody is looking after everybody. I will develop the issue further later on.

Now…

Let's face our truth.

•

Contemplation

Close your eyes.
Enter into a meditative state.
Breathe deeply a few times.
Contact your heart.
Listen to your inner silence.

Ask yourself:

"From where do I live my life?"

"Do I act solely to satisfy my own personal desires? To satisfy my selfishness?"

"Do I act to give the best of myself? Do I always seek the greatest good for everybody?"

There is no judgment here. We are not judging anyone. You are here to learn and to advance... wherever you are.

Write down your answers and look at them from time to time, and take a decision to change what is needed.

THE ONLY OPTION: SERVICE

> *"The result of*
> *service is joy."*

The issue of compassion takes us to another big issue in life. In life, there is only one thing: Service. Service to love and service with love is the highest way to live. This is the New Humanity, the new consciousness. "Service is a path to enlightenment and peace," like a friend said. "...Selfless service is like a river that takes us to the sea of perfection and plenitude. Interested service is no service at all; it is like a dry river. It is useless."

When we talk of service, we talk of serving a greater cause. This is living not only for "yourself," in the sense that what you do only benefits you, and it is aimed at your own satisfaction. Service is offering yourself, your life, your talents, what you have and what you are, to life in whatever form it presents itself. It is an offering to God from you, from what He has given you. And you do it through offering it to others. Does that mean you don't look after yourself or after your life? Of course not. You do all that you need to do and want to do, to expand your personal situation, life, power, wealth, abilities, consciousness and everything else… but making it an act of service. This is serving your higher purpose and this too, needs to be done, but from this greater perspective: the perspective that it is service.

See God. He is serving all the time everything, everybody. Not only is He the sustainer of all life every second of eternity, He does not take a break or a holiday from it. There is only one way in the Universe: Service. There is only service in life; everything else is going nowhere. This is the way to happiness.

THE MESSAGE OF AQUARIUS

Aquarius has a symbol: the water bearer. He carries an amphora on his shoulder. He pours water, gives of the acknowledgment of his own abundance – unlimited one. Because he, manifested as a human being, is one with the Divine Source. He is a channel for God's Grace and abundance. His abundance comes from Him, hence his amphora never runs dry. His is a message of serving. This is what the Violet Light is about.

•

Feel the infinite bounty of God Source, pouring down on you as a cascade of Violet Light. See this light pouring out from you into the world."

– CHAPTER 7 –

•

RISING TO YOUR INNER TRUTH

"Because you are light,
you are peace now."
– The Ascended Masters

VIBRATION: THE KEY TO ALL DOORS

It is very important that we, as human beings, realize a fact of life and start living with it:

"Everything is vibration."

The importance of this cannot be underestimated. On it depends what you are and what happens to you every moment of your life. Its importance is as dramatic as to say that the way you vibrate determines what people, events and destiny you attract to you and to your life. Hence your vibration determines your karma. What should be clear here, is that the better you vibrate the better things will be for you, in absolute terms. To vibrate well means to vibrate high.

Life is all energy and energy vibrates, as we saw earlier on. So you can change anything by changing its vibration. Since all energy vibrates, the key to energy is vibration. Since life is all energy, the key to life is also vibration, and the mastery of vibration is the mastery of life. If you understand this, you have the key to life's secrets.

If you vibrate high, you attract prosperity and you issue a response of love to life. If you vibrate low, you attract problems: you issue a response of fear to life. In a way we have seen this. But...

How do you vibrate high?

You have to think positively, love yourself, love others, have faith, smile, be kind, generous, peaceful... This is where the problem starts. If you were like this all the time, you would be all right. You would experience prosperity all the time, spiritual and material prosperity. But how do you keep there all the time? Mostly the way to do it, is working your mind with your mind to make the necessary effort to be alert to change, to create and to stay in those states of positive awareness. But then the quality of the work falls: you have your human nature to deal with, which is not really trained to stay there all the time. So the good work is lost and with it the vibration. So you have to start again.

It is easier to do it the other way around:

"Instead of trying to attain those positive states to have a high vibration, have a high vibration to attain those states."

There are energies of high vibration that if you tap into them, can create those states for you spontaneously. An energy like this is the Violet Light. This light keeps you in high vibration because it is stronger than those tendencies to vibrate low. In practical terms this means that in connecting to the Violet Light, you acquire a high vibration that allows you to spontaneously generate those positive attitude states mentioned above. The Violet Light has the power to burn all negativity from your heart and mind, then it manifests the high vibration necessary to create those higher states in you. As you become purified with this light, increasingly those positive attitudes will be generated naturally in you without effort.

God manifests Himself as a Universal force through vibration. This vibration has a universal reference: the well-known "OM." From this Universal Force, Creation manifests itself. "OM" has been known through ages as the primordial vibration: the vibration from which all others come from. It is not a mere mantra that Tibetan Lamas or other followers of meditation repeat for their practices, as we have all heard at some point. It is a vibration – a sound – which can in fact be heard in deep meditation spontaneously. So it is there pulsating constantly. OM is one of the ways the principle of vibration of the Universe can be identified. Another is light.

The principle of vibration doesn't change all the way from the purest state of God, to the workings of this physical world. This fact has not been altered through time or space, or any world that has been created, including the world we live in. The principle of vibration is fully operative every second of our lives, every instant of existence. It doesn't make any difference to it if we ignore it, or whether it is taught in schools, universities or in the church, and the fact that it is not, at least not directly, doesn't change its reality. In fact the Bible in its sentence: "At the beginning was the Word," makes a coded reference to this universal sound, to the principle of vibration, as the origin of everything. We can step down and understand from this, that vibration is the origin of everything, the seed that manifests reality in whatever form it takes. Since every thought, feeling, word and action have a vibration, they generate life. According to the quality of their vibration, they will generate one thing or another. A good healthy seed of wheat will generate a good ear of wheat; a bad one will create a poor quality plant. What confers the quality to words you say or actions you perform, is the intention behind them. That intention will instill a vibration in them.

When words or actions are performed with love, they have the vibration of love and generate a good crop. It is often difficult for human beings to act in this way. Love is not a real value in this material world – it certainly does not rank in the stock exchange. Since the human heart is so wounded, often its creation is one of suffering and fear instead of one of love and peace. So actions, words, feelings are sent out into the field of life to create harvests of delusion, disappointment and disaster. The human heart needs to be healed, purified. This is the work of the Violet Light. When the Violet Light enters into a person, it purifies the heart restoring its ability to

65

love. Then the actions, words, feelings that a person sends out will generate the best harvest – the positive results and beneficial outcomes we all desire in our lives.

So whether you know it or not, the principle of vibration is still ruling your life. So better get to grips with it and start using it consciously to create the life you want. What is relevant for us here in order to use this understanding, is to see that vibration rules. Know that you, created as image of the Great Spirit, have the same creative power through vibration. This creative power manifests in your life through the way you vibrate. If you are a positive person, motivated, inspired in life, you will be vibrating in a positive way and will attract to your life positive people, events and circumstances. If you feel depressed, nothing motivates you and you have negative thoughts, your gloomy attitude will create a low frequency that will manifest as negative vibration, attracting to you negative people, events and circumstances. The principle in both cases is the same: vibration. When you increase your vibration, the inferior frequencies don't affect you. Some of those are the ones of your own ego: selfishness, anger, pride, fear, that can also come from others. You are really protected in the light, love, and power higher vibration brings. The inferior frequencies can't touch you because you vibrate above them – unless they go to you to be uplifted. This happens too.

We could even say: health = high vibration; illness = low vibration. Inner peace = high vibration; negativity = low vibration. Essentially:

Vibration = consciousness
High vibration = high consciousness

A high vibration always governs over inferior vibrations, it has more energy and therefore more power, love and action. Understanding all these workings of the Universe and therefore of your own life, you can see the precious value of having an agent of high vibration in your hands like the Violet Light. With a key like this to change the vibration of things, there is nothing stopping you evolving and changing your universe in the most appropriate way. The Violet Light as such high vibration, deconstructs all structures. It changes the laws of energies and their behavior. This light is not limited by any reality. Since it has the power to elevate beings spiritually and dissolve their karma, it is changing the rules and creating new realities. The Violet Light therefore makes the rules wherever it manifests.

The Violet Light as a source of high vibration raises your energy and expands your consciousness.

Expanded consciousness means:

♥   Inner peace
♥   Love
♥   Service attitude = selflessness
♥   Clarity
♥   Freedom
♥   True power
♥   Abundance
♥   Transmutation of karmas
♥   Spirituality
♥   Revelation of our inner being or True Self
♥   Union with God
♥   Ascension

So the key mantra for this age is:

"Vibrate High"

RECOVERING YOUR TRUE IDENTITY: YOUR LUMINOUS SELF

"I Am" is not just the present form of "To Be." This is the vibration of your Inner Self, which is also called: Christ Self or Higher Self. It is equivalent to the "Buddha state" depending on your spiritual background. This really is your "Luminous Self." Words here are relative: we are talking about Universal realities. So don't let words limit you. The consciousness of that state is one in which you see yourself in everything, and recognize that you not only exist here where your body and mind are, but also in everything and in everyone: in all life.

This state of the Luminous Self has been spoken about in all spiritual traditions. The Hindu tradition has a well-known mantra, "So Ham" which means precisely "I Am." The Metaphysical tradition often speaks of the mighty inner presence as "I Am" or "I Am Presence." This is the same Jesus often talks about when he says: "I am the resurrection and the life." In other spiritual traditions there are terms that mean exactly the same. Jesus also refers to it when he says in the Bible that he and His Father are one, because it is through the Luminous Self that this is possible. He also shows his Luminous Self in his Transfiguration.

The relevance of talking about this here, is that you should know this is your real state of being, but most probably you do not experience it, at least not fully. Due to our separation from the Divine Source, and to our state of ignorance about what we really are, we live cut off from experiencing our own Divinity to the full. Then the Luminous Self remains largely ignored throughout life. The power of the Violet Light takes you to experience your "I Am" presence progressively, as it removes your limits, those wrong illusory perceptions of yourself in separation, by deleting them from your consciousness. Then you can access your Luminous Self.

•

"It is a good practice to close your eyes for a few minutes in a quiet moment, and to observe your breathing consciously. As you do so, say inwardly: "I AM" as you breathe in, and again "I AM" as you breathe out. This simple practice done regularly will activate the serenity awareness of your Luminous Self."

•

When I was sixteen I found myself in the state of the Luminous Self. I wrote spiritual poetry, which came to me in very inspired states. One day the inspiration was so strong that I kept going higher and higher within myself. My vibration was rising up and suddenly my consciousness took a jump and I merged into it: everything before me was "me." I recognized myself in everything, the sky, the houses, the trees. I was as much my own self, as I was everything else. It was amazing. There were some things that came with that state. The most impressive was a shocking knowledge that I already knew that state is what I am – an impacting recovery of my spiritual memory. I kept saying: "I knew it," "I knew it." I also felt an ecstatic bliss far beyond anything that could be imagined. I had the deep experience that I was everything.

I can tell you from this experience that the "I Am" state is not a nice story spiritual paths or religions talk about; it is the reality. The transcendence of our existence is far beyond what we imagine in our daily lives. We are power, love and wisdom without limits. These are the main attributes of the "I Am" presence: the Luminous Self. But we live believing in limits, death, lack and illness, suffering and unworthiness, when we are God Himself in essence. The Violet Light is here to transmute that wrong perception and limited beliefs about ourselves, and to return to us our state of complete freedom that is our right as sons of God.

69

I have seen this effect of the light happening to so many people during and after the Violet Light courses. Negative thinking, destructive attitudes, lack of harmony, lack of love, despair, all those states start to be liberated from the person. Also they experience profound inner and outer changes for the best. Nonetheless, work needs to be kept up by the individual, but with the help of this light each person is placed in his perfect state of harmony, clarity and empowerment – his highest positive state – where the realization of all the aspects of the inner personal potential are possible to the highest degree. This is why in the promotion of the Violet Light courses, we often use the message that clearly says what we can do with this energy:

**"Transmute your karma,
Create your destiny."**

– CHAPTER 8 –

•

HOW IT WORKS

*"When your mind understands
that it needs the light of God,
it will be your ally."*
– Jesus and The Masters

LIBERATION

There is no secret about this. As a human being, you want to become free of the weight of pain, suffering, limitations, ignorance... all that which is not the true essence of your Luminous Self.

The key word here is: **Ascension**.

In freeing ourselves from that unwanted weight we go up like a balloon – we ascend. In ascending we become free. This is the goal which we are all aiming at: spiritual illumination – to experience and to live in the awareness of the Luminous Self. So through this liberation we access the Eternal in us, and we can live from there an experience of life free of pain and full of joy and peace. Liberation is to become completely free from the attachment to what is ephemeral in our lives. Notice that I said "from the attachment" not "from the things." Why? Because the attachments are the weights that stop us, they are the obstacles to live a full life. They keep us tied and it is those bonds that make us suffer when they break against our will. The influence of the Violet Light takes us through a liberation of all that neurotic attachment, to a new freedom. Then it is possible to live without worry. Due to the power in action of the Violet Light and the alchemical quality of this energy, the main activity by which it is known is that of...

TRANSMUTATION

From the alchemists' point of view, base metal becomes gold through an alchemical process. We have seen this in the section "Alchemy." This process of change in vibration alchemy sought is called:

"Transmutation"

Transmutation can be best explained as the transformation of something into its best possibility. For us the "base metal" of the ego has to become the "gold" of the spiritual Self. This transmutation requires of an immensely powerful energy. The alchemical process of it, takes everything from the state in which it is, to the best state in which it can be. This is the essence of the alchemical activity of the Violet Light.

In the tradition of many cultures there is the "mythical figure," which is the beacon of light religions and civilizations follow as a path to the goal of life. We will develop this in detail in the section "Final Vision:" "Personal Myth." That mythical figure be it a saint like Jesus or a mystic magician like Merlin, becomes mythical through the invocation and influence of a superior energy, that transforms him completely from his merely humane condition to his divine potential. It is from that state beyond the ordinary manifestation of Man, that mythical figures wield their so called powers of magic and miracle, as well as, and really what this is all about, their loving radiation and their ecstatic attitude, from where they magnetize all life and others to their compelling presence. The realization of the personal myth in each of us is the goal of life: the discovery and manifestation of all the unconsciously divine potential and all that it carries with it. But there has to be that alchemical process to get to it. That assistance can only come from above in any of some possible ways. It is a force of tremendous power, love and light. Without it, the human remains human and Quetzalcoatl never flies. Thus, a human being never realizes the full spiritual potential hidden latent in his or her being. It is through this force that Jesus becomes the Christ, that Prince Siddharta becomes Buddha, and Quetzalcoatl the winged serpent – the Christ of the Aztec culture. In Mayan culture too, transmutation is beautifully represented by that winged serpent, which as an ordinary reptile lives closely attached to the ground, but when it develops wings becomes a higher being and can be compared to an eagle or an angel. It is the god "Kukulcan," Mayan people's own Christ figure, which at the spring equinox "casts" a serpent shadow on the main pyramid of "Chichen Itza," in Mexican Mayan land. That very valid symbol is comparable to what happens to any man, who is touched by the superior, transforming energy of the Violet Light.

NOTHING STAYS...

I said before that liberation was to become free from attachment, but also from dependency. God is independence, and everything that means dependency is not of God. One of the effects of the Violet Light is the transmutation of your attachment and desire for what is non-permanent, giving you greater independence. In that way it gives you the consciousness that transforms your mind, for you to differentiate clearly that which is permanent from that which is not – in order to free yourself from the obsessive grip the non-permanent things have on you. This means you enjoy the ephemeral things but do not become so obsessively attached to them, and therefore so dependent on them. In fact you then enjoy them more fully and with more freedom. You need greater light in you for this. This light brings more clarity. With that clarity you can dedicate more time of your life to know, explore, have more communion with and live in contact with the everlasting reality. This is a contrast with the general life of human beings on this planet, that dedicate all or most of their lives to entertain that which is ephemeral, thus becoming deeply attached to it. Being more in contact with the undying reality has the obvious result of a more peaceful life, full of inner meaning, stability and purpose.

We as human beings live as if the temporary things were going to last forever. If you attach yourself excessively to the transitory things, what happens? Think about it for a moment. You treat them as if they were going to last forever. And when they don't, what happens? You suffer. If you are honest with yourself, you will see this was the case in the many times something left you, and you suffered as a result of it. Then you cry, there is pain, you believe that a part of yourself is dying. Why? The problem lies in your false sense of identity which you have about yourself, which I mentioned earlier on. From it you draw a sense of identity out of the ephemeral: possessions, the body, work, profession, status, opinions, affiliations, nationality, friends, partners, children, likes, dislikes, house, car, appearance and so on. You decided at some point along the way, that all those things and more are what "you are." Then whenever any of those things changes or goes away, you enter into crisis because you firmly believe "what you are" is being threatened. You drew an identity from them. Then they go... you feel like dying. The feeling of dying is illusory. But it looks real to you from that wrong perspective of the association you made with the transient reality.

The truth is that those ephemeral things you associate with, are going to go anyway, because all that which is transient sooner or later disappears – only that you never welcomed the time for that, and when it arrives, it invariably takes you by surprise. You deceived yourself into thinking it was never going to happen. This is the attachment that leads to suffering, depression and other similar things. What do you do? Here you need a change in perspective, to treat the transient for what it is: non-permanent, and to treat the everlasting for what it is: permanent. Then you also need to develop a true sense of identity, of what you "truly are" as a human being, which is done by getting into a good relationship with your Luminous Self. To do this you need very clear self-observation, in order to discern what is permanent from what is not. And then live with that knowledge, treating each one consequently and also seeing what your mind is doing with both. The Violet Light helps you deeply in developing this

74

awareness. Just by practicing the meditations in this book, you will find that the light will create a different mental and spiritual frame for you, which will start to free you from all those excessive attachments that you have, on the path towards your freedom and peace. The Violet Light acts as a great dissolvent of all those dependent approaches to life, without you needing to worry about whether it is going to work for you, or understanding the way it does. Gravity works. The sun shines for everyone, regardless of whether we understand the way it works. The Violet Light has its own divine power: it acts by itself without your intervention. It is Divine Intelligence.

•

Contemplation

Let's go inside for a few minutes.

Breathe deeply... allow yourself to fall into your heart.

Ask yourself in silence:

What is there in my life which is permanent?
Where do I live from, the greatest part of my time?
Do I live in touch with the everlasting?
...or in touch with the temporary?
Do I remember God or my Luminous Self enough?

Allow time for the answers to come. Face the truth about them.
Do not hide them or give excuses for what is. This is a work of
self change. You need total honesty.

When you are ready, bring yourself out of the contemplation breathing deeply a couple of times. If you wish make a note of your answers for your present and future reference.

•

It is amazing to realize for oneself, how little time of our day we dedicate to being in touch with the permanent reality of life. The Sufis call it: "Absent-mindedness of God." If we understand the fact that whatever we are concentrated upon, that we become impregnated of, it would be of no surprise to see why we suffer so much and have the kind of traumatic experiences and disappointments we do have in this world. Buddha said: "existence is suffering," referring to the ordinary existence in the ephemeral world. The truth is that without a good connection and relationship with the enduring reality of life, we are weak and life is nearer to that first principle of Buddha for us, than to the Nirvana – the permanent blissful state which he attained. After devoting the necessary effort and time, Buddha reached the experience of the eternal and thus the freedom from the relative world where suffering lies.

"This world is a farce, do not believe in it."

"What happens outside is completely irrelevant."

– Jesus

In this recent message Jesus refers to the world as the apparent reality we live in, which is not real because it is ephemeral. So Buddha and Jesus are saying essentially the same. In these two sentences Jesus clearly says that what truly matters is what happens inside oneself, the part that never dies. He is saying that the world outside is an illusory one, a world of change – ephemeral world – that does not deserve all the excessive attention and importance we give it. But that the world inside, which is the one that truly matters, is not cared for enough. A world where the true meaning of life lies, where the important things take place, where the biggest decisions are made. Decisions out of our thoughts, feelings and motivations, all that which creates Karma and therefore the way our lives will go. That's why he said: "It is not what enters the mouth of man what defiles him, it is what comes out of him

76

instead," meaning that what comes out – words, intentions – comes from the heart. If that heart is not open, full of love and compassion it will bring suffering and chaos to the person. So it is not surprising that what matters is inside, and what that inside manifests outside will depend on its quality.

So we can conclude…

When you balance something with the Violet Light, it liberates blockages and karmas, anything impeding the manifestation of the Presence – Love, Will and Consciousness – of God, directly and without interferences. This manifestation of the Will of God is the most natural thing; it is in fact the real state of everything when liberated from disharmony. In the Violet Light there is that Divine Presence, that intention, that Will of God.

●

"Enter into a moment of quietness now.
From the top of your head "see" a
beam of Violet Light going to heaven.
Feel that you and God are one."

– CHAPTER 9 –

•

MIDWAY STATION:
FORGIVENESS & FREEDOM

> *"The unity of all hearts in the light,*
> *is the key that opens the door."*
> – Kahan

So far, we have traveled through the universe of a wonderful energy that perhaps you have noticed flies on the wings of freedom. All we have seen about the Violet Light has to do with freedom – a freedom we all look for – elusive and truly unknown to most people, yet always present in the deepest dreams of any man's heart. We have been talking of your freedom and about the liberation of mankind. Now we will see one of the key aspects of this.

The first truth we have to consider here, is that there is no freedom without forgiveness. This takes us to look into the subject of forgiveness in a different way, than what we are used to. Most people look at forgiveness as a choice they can consciously make, an option life offers and through their "free" will, make that option a reality in their lives. But, is it really a choice we can make? How free are we to take that choice fully? Perhaps forgiving is a choice we have taken many times, but how successful have we been at it? For, if it is not a permanent release, it is not real. If we keep remembering the deed and still have feelings about it, our forgiving has not been successful. These are some of the points we can make about one of the keys to life, because the truth is that, if you do not release through forgiving, you are tied up to hurt, resentment and finally to fatal illness. If in order to be free you have to forgive, then if you don't you are choosing limitation and imprisonment. But let me show you that all I have said about this makes all the sense.

DIFFICULT TO FORGIVE?

Forgiveness happens in the heart. When you go to the heart, if it has not been purified the first thing you encounter is pain. A layer of pain and suffering covers the heart with an accumulation of old hurts, that have not been resolved nor released. In the attempt to open to forgive, you find you cannot. It seems to hurt to forgive, so we don't do it – at least not properly most of the time. So what do we do? Putting off that opening gives time power, since what is not released today will be more difficult tomorrow. The later we leave it the more crystallized those old habits will be, and to allow something that has to be done sooner or later "sleep," will make the mind become lazier and eventually it will end up refusing to do it. Then Karma comes. It is hard to understand for the average human condition, that forgiveness is the way. The first primal reaction of the ego, is to get back or to get even. But the average human condition is not very good at understanding the larger reality of life. That takes extra effort, and to dare to walk other not so popular paths – since they take people away from the sleepy comfort of an unconscious, but otherwise painful life. It supposes more effort, those paths are not so available and to walk them presupposes to face oneself, and that is not precisely comfortable most of the time.

But opening the heart is not only the way to forgive truly: it is the only way to live a sane, meaningful life. Before finding true love, the heart has to be purified. It has to be released from everything that has got stuck to it, in order to avoid being hurt again – thus covering that love. That was a survival choice, but a tricky one. Perhaps when it happened to most of us, we did not know other more enlightened choices, but being the wrong one it created the karma we eventually have to face. The true problem here is that vision is not in the eyes. Vision is in the heart. Therefore what you see, what you perceive in life depends on the state of your heart. If the heart is covered by those layers, we are short sighted. If the heart is full of sadness, we will see a sad world. If it is full of fear, the vision will be that of a terrifying world. A heart full of resentment, judges and condemns the world. If you have a heart full of love, you will see a loving world. When we forgive we access unity, then the door opens to greater treasures for all.

The path therefore is:

Purifying the heart

The vision:

Innocence

But how can we do it if we see through judging eyes, eyes that see condemnation? Here is where the Violet Energy comes to play.

INNOCENCE: A NEW VISION

> *"God's Will is perfect happiness for me.*
> *And I can suffer but from the belief*
> *there is another will apart from His."*
> – A Course in Miracles

We have said that the typical reaction when somebody hurts us is that of retaliation, judgment, rejection. True compassion would be a better response but we are not seeing what is there, we only see our pain. To elicit such a response we have to truly see what is there – not our judgments. To change your vision of hurtful events is not easy without assistance. Therefore it is important to recognize the need of help. The Violet Light is a powerful help in cleansing the heart of past pain that blocks our vision and love, allowing you to open up to a new vision of things: the vision of innocence. With that help, and your own effort, you can achieve a lot since you are welcoming a power greater than yourself. Then you understand that the projection of pain through criticism, judgment and condemnation was keeping you blind. You begin to see the innocence in yourself and in people who were confused by fear, people needing love and acceptance so afraid of loneliness they could not function properly. So threatened by the projection of their own insecurities and fears, they thought they had to be aggressive with the world to protect their own supposed weakness, and therefore denied close ones a love they actually felt and needed to give and receive.

In the Violet Light courses, there is a part where we go into meditation to contact hurtful events of our past. We will see about it later on. After the experience, people often report having seen the situation with new eyes. Sometimes people are able to contact and feel the hurt they blocked for so long... something opens up – the heart – and they cry deep tears of liberation or enter into catharsis. At other times, they see the situation without being touched by the emotional charge, for the first time. The Violet Light allows them a detachment from the situation and a healing of the pain. Through that, the perception of the traumatic event is changed for a vision of forgiveness and release. It is such a joy for me to see them liberated. It is such a relief from their burdens that their hearts sing with gratitude. That is what really pays for the work I do. When I see such powerful effects, I am in awe at the Violet Light once again, recognizing unmistakably the power of God through the Holy Spirit, in the form of this sacred light.

MERCY AND FORGIVENESS

It is time we seek help, and it is right to do so. Help from the only place it can come: from above. God is not by any means a judging presence. If we really knew that, we would go to Him more often. Isn't this true of yourself? It has been one of the greatest conclusions I have reached after years of deep spiritual practice and inner contemplation, to realize that God is an immense benevolent force. The solution to all the issues of life rests in Him. The problems lie in a disconnection from that beautiful source of power and goodness; this is when we fall into trouble. He is not doing more in your or anybody's life, because He is not allowed to. He has given you free will: you make your choices. What would be the point of giving you free will if He made the choices for you? Bad choices therefore lead to suffering. Karma is the way we learn.

The law of God and of life is Love. To live against that, is a bad choice. So He is not to blame for the problems or unbalances of your life, you are. If you want the best help, I advise you to seek His. This is also an exercise of your free will. I am here to tell you this, and to let you know that one of the greatest helps He has ever offered mankind, is here right now in the form of the Violet Light.

The poor relationship you might have with God, is not with Him, it is with the wrong idea of Him you have developed. In fact the relationship He has with you is excellent, or else you would be wiped out of existence this very second. He sustains all creation constantly. He is the Universal Creating Force and the Universal Sustaining Force. Therefore He has everything you might need. You have His help for eternity. That is what Mercy is: help from God. The power of that Mercy can free you from whatever difficult situation you might have fallen into. Think for a moment… if there is a force that can free you from a limiting condition without asking conditions, wouldn't that be… forgiveness? Let's use other more slippery terms… "to absolve you," "to redeem you," Forgiveness, in its greatest state, don't we call it… Mercy?

So we have arrived at common terms but through a different path. This is the truth: He has the power, He grants the Grace, He asks nothing in return, you and I receive the blessings, the benefit. We become free: we are forgiven. One form of that Mercy has now a distinct violet color…

The color of freedom

The liberation of Karma takes a human being to the experience of love. This individual liberation in which you are redeemed is from where you can forgive. Since there are two parts in forgiveness:

- The forgiving of yourself
- The forgiving you grant your fellow beings

One is necessary to exercise the other. But how do you go about forgiving yourself, when there is so much pain covering the heart? The difficulty in forgiving someone is that we have not forgiven ourselves. When you find it difficult to forgive, it is because you don't see innocence in another, you don't believe in his innocence. You don't see it, because you don't see yours. As we judge ourselves, we also judge others. So finally everything comes down to the forgiveness God bestows upon us, because if we have accepted the forgiveness of God over us, we will be able to forgive others.

God sees you perfect, but you don't. So what is needed is that you change the way you see yourself. This is forgiveness. It is hard to do it most of the time. This is why you need help. As you are helped with the Violet Light the judging and condemning attitude and the hardness you have towards yourself are loosened and you enter into a state of relaxed acceptance as your way of living. You then feel very different about yourself. It is such a relief to experience it; you feel all weight is taken away from you. Then you take away the weight of your judging – your disapproving vision of others. But first you are being helped to become free. If you can forgive others, you have forgiven yourself.

Through the Violet Light this is possible. As you meditate and work with it on the liberation of your karmas and blockages, it will become more and more obvious and you will experience greater freedom in yourself. This will result in greater peace, an unequivocal sign that you are getting nearer to God Consciousness. As you see yourself blessed with greater freedom, you will be able to forgive things that you could not until then, because you yourself have been redeemed by the action of the Light. Therefore your vision of others will change to one of greater understanding. Along the way, a deep and true feeling of love for all human beings will increase naturally in you, and the ability to live from an open loving heart that spills compassion, sweetness and support for all life, will become real. This means that there is communion with the divine inside you. The Violet Light has entered you and it has blessed you enough, to free you form the old vision of guilt and punishment, providing you with a new freedom. In one word: it helps you to see the color of freedom. Violet is the color of freedom, as Master Saint Germain has said many times, associating the state of freedom from karmas to the action of the Violet Light. In His book, "The Golden Book," he actually defines the Violet Light as the "Law of forgiveness." The Violet Light is in this way the power of Mercy to its greatest potential.

Through the action of the Violet Light upon all your bodies, physical, emotional, mental and spiritual, there is a great change that takes place. These redemption takes form in two possible ways. The first one: you might be redeemed of something completely straight away. The second: some parts of the issue will be redeemed immediately, the rest will take some time, but it will involve patience and to keep working with the Grace the Violet Light brought you. That is why there is a section of practices later on.

Note

I want to make an important clarification here. I am talking in general terms, when I say that the Violet Light can change or redeem any situation or circumstances in your life. This is true as far as your life circumstances and relationships with work, people, environment and so on, and includes your spiritual evolution in the ways described so far. As far as helping with personal suffering, I refer to mental and emotional suffering. With regard to physical damage that involves chronic or acute critical conditions, things can be helped but due to the acuteness of it, the improvement can be very slow and perhaps will not be seen in this life. As far as irreversible physical damage as a result of a external influence, cannot be included here. Because this implies extreme deterioration to organs or physical structure. Structural damage is almost impossible to be redressed, with the physical bodies we have now. Acutely ill internal organs although difficult to heal, can be improved, but it might not be noticeable to the person or it might not reached the point to improve his or her life quality. Due to the karmic weight physical structural damage implies, most of those conditions cannot be redressed in the same lifetime. So consider the Mercy of God available through the Violet Light taking into account this point. We all know the most amazing miracles can happen, but only God knows how, when and where.

•

THE WAY TO PEACE

Peace is in that communion with the Divine. Away from this, there is no peace. It is God, divinity itself when awakened inside a man that radiates peace as his inner state. That awakening is granted by the Violet Light, and if it has already taken place in the person by other means, such individual is promoted to higher realms of spiritual realization, and with it to the deep experience of permanent peace. Peace is already there – but we do not experience it. This is because it is covered by thoughts and emotions, beliefs and attitudes that oppose peace: they resonate in negativity. Instead of the natural peace inside, what is lived are those layers of the mind, producing an experience of unrest. These are the layers of disharmony that the Violet Light dissolves, cleaning the way for you to experience that inner peace within.

High energy moves all other energies, it "rules" over them. It dismantles them resulting in greater peace for you. It is the energies of no peace in you that have to be removed, or else you will experience their vibrations: hatred, resentment, pain, fear... how can you experience peace with them? The Mercy of God is above any law. The Mercy of God comes from the Holy Spirit. There is nothing more powerful than the Holy Spirit. The Holy Spirit when invoked is the one that solves all situations. The Violet Light as a form of the Holy Spirit of God has the power of forgiveness, as it offers the liberation of any condition that is away from perfection, restoring the consciousness of any individual to his natural state of bliss, peace and divine power, thus providing a reconnection with the Universal Power Source. This is the liberation this Divine Light offers you:

Liberation: from it to peace

It is when a human being awakens to his spiritual reality, that he becomes transformed into a being of love, a compassionate being. A man like this experiences prosperity in all areas of his life, since he has been released, and he himself has released the past. In that liberation energy flow is restored and since the past has been freed, there is movement forward. Holdbacks have been removed and therefore prosperity in all areas – from the top to the bottom, from spiritual to material – is manifested. So forgiveness is linked to the greater idea of prosperity, that which God Himself embodies. If there is no prosperity there cannot be real peace.

Purification and Peace

You need to understand that the only one who can purify your heart is God – His Holy Spirit. The Violet Light purifies your heart because it raises the vibration of everything that is not harmonious in it, healing it: erasing guilt and the suffering it brings; removing blockages to love. As people avoid forgiving, they lose their energy. Life energy comes from the Universal Source. In not forgiving they become disconnected from the Source, because the source of life does not judge, it does not see guilt; it only sees innocence in all. So in that disconnection one is blocking the Source and therefore loses life energy. One ages because one does not forgive. Then one becomes rigid, ill; one suffers.

Basically when something wrong happens and you have to forgive, you may find that you want justice to be done. Purification is pending. Avoiding forgiveness is maintaining judgments. There is no peace in this attitude. What has to happen is release, this is done by purifying the heart. Justice is for God. He is the one who knows what should be done and how. You just forgive. The way is to enter into love and to forgive your brother for his error. This is the way you will find peace. As you leave justice to God, you are released from a burden that was making your life miserable. A burden you cannot carry because it is not yours. Justice is in God's hands. The Violet Light helps you with that difficulty. It helps you at that which until now was probably so traumatic and so difficult to let go, so that you become free from it and can enter into peace finally.

•

"Close your eyes for a moment. See
the Violet Grace entering your body,
your heart, your mind. See it all illumined
in its forgiveness. Feel this experience.

FORGIVENESS BEFORE JUDGMENT

Forgiveness gives you the correct vision. Through it, you see that the person doing wrong actions is in suffering and pain. He is actually full of fear. It is fundamental to stop seeing oneself as being victim of pain and suffering. This is to give your power outside. Judgment, condemnation, and punishment do not free you. They are only desires of vengeance. Evil has to be cast away in the heart. Those things only poison you. In order to manifest the correct vision it is necessary not to react from negative ego, or from its desire to get back when something wrong happens. Avoiding having a condemning reaction from the ego, we do to others what we want to be done to ourselves. In doing it, we have forgiven because we have not entered into the attack and defense mode. What we wrongly call justice is our thirst for vengeance. We have seen we leave justice to God. He is the one directing the Universe, not us. We are not in condition to administer it. He is, if He wills. We leave that work to Him. Our function is to remain in peace through forgiving, since forgiving purifies us and allows us to see the Truth. You then, as an individual, do not see anymore someone attacking you, you see someone in fear, someone suffering, someone fighting with his ghosts; basically someone in need. The only thing you can do then is placing things right inside yourself and let the Will of God manifest. This might mean you have to take some action, or it might mean to stay still.

It all comes down to guilt. The original sin is really that of guilt – we all see ourselves as guilty, so what can we see from there? Guilt. We see our fellow beings guilty, and everyone sees a world of guilty people which is a world without peace, a world of separation and suffering. That is why it is so important to develop the attitude of:

"Forgiveness before judgment"

Forgiveness is an inner act of letting go. It does not mean that we forgive to benefit the other. That power is in God. You forgive so that you do not hold anything against your brother. It is for you, it is your liberation. We do not have the power to judge. If we do not free, we will not be set free, as Jesus said in many ways.

Jesus said:

"Forgive them Father for they do not know what they are doing."

He did not judge them. He saw their innocence as God always does.

Our own forgiveness

We need to understand that our own forgiveness cannot be outside ourselves. Otherwise it would mean that there is a power of judgment outside. This would imply that other beings can judge us and condemn us, with a different will to God's Will. God does not judge us, He always sees our innocence. To place forgiveness outside ourselves would be to give our power away. And that is not a law of God. The believe in placing the power outside is the way some people created to control humanity. This is the purpose of guilt. And with it there is the need to be absolved. So you have to find someone or something to grant you absolution. Through this way a great system for controlling people's power has been developed. Our power is inside in our unity with the Creator. If this was not so, it would place some beings nearer to God and above the rest of humans, and this is not the case. The law that balances everything is the Law of Karma, what Jesus called: "As you sow, so shall you reap." God sees all. The Law of Karma is in action all the time. There is no need for judges. Everyone gets exactly what they deserve from their actions.

This does not mean that if you need the help of someone able to grant it to you, as a means of counseling, healing or helping you see the way to the light, you don't seek it. You must seek help if you need it. But no one is going to absolve you other than God. If you are suffering from the torture of guilt, or cannot find relief from the burden of your own judgment, do seek help immediately so you can be lead to the path of absolution in God. In any case prayer and

90

meditation will take you back to the right path and will help you find your inner peace. You can always ask God for help and to a sincere seeker it will always be granted. And the good thing is that people can pray and ask blessings for others. We all can and should do it.

The truth is that we are independent of human powers and systems, because we have the power of God inside – the power of good and the power of correction. Dependency does not work. This is not what Jesus and other Masters taught. He taught that everything is between oneself and God without intermediaries that administrate His power – and therefore His forgiveness. He proclaimed spiritual independence. And this has not been understood yet. In His work "A Course in Miracles," one of the most powerful spiritual teachings ever written, there is a section called: "Do not look outside yourself" where Jesus explains it is all inside. If everything is inside forgiveness must also be inside. And inside, there is God. Every time we look for completion outside ourselves, we create an idol. An idol is there to grant us its power, so we believe. This way we become dependent and therefore weak. Man has created idols of forgiveness through which he would feel absolved of his sins… by a power outside. Then idols are worshiped with great veneration, since they "have" the power of absolution, undoubtedly granted to them by Man. No idol or figure outside you has the power to grant you forgiveness. In essence, no one is closer to God than you. Repentance is inside. It is something between you and God. He is the one to be accountable to. We put an idol in the place where we should put God. An idol will always say "yes" in granting its power, it wants you back so that you keep giving your power to it.

The only true and safe place to put our trust is in God. He is the one to pray for the forgiveness of our faults, and He will give us the consciousness and the wisdom to live better lives. The place to go to, is the place where true power is, from there we can obtain it: the Divine Source. We have to act from the consciousness of creating the world we want for us and for others. This blesses you and all.

A NEW BEGINNING...

The aim of this section was to agree with you on some basic truths, and to support you in solving the difficulty of forgiving fully.

Forgiveness brings you:

- More energy
- Peace
- Health – physical, emotional, mental
- Communion with your Divine Self
- Liberation of Karma
- Spiritual elevation
- Prosperity
- Opportunities
- Harmony
- Love
- Power

Therefore we can agree that it is necessary to forgive.

In a book which is read at the energy level like this one, you want to find experience – not just mere words – and the experience of forgiveness is what the Violet Light brings you. You can see the difficulty in forgiving yourself and others. My assistance to you in this, is to offer you the presence of the Violet Light. To make that assistance stronger at this point, you can do the following meditation.

First consider this:

The Violet Light helps you to see your innocence and that of your brother. It assists you in having compassion. It helps you enter into peace. It rejuvenates you because it opens your heart.

Receive it all in this:

"Liberation of pending issues"

- *Sit down in your special place.*

- *You can light a candle and an incense stick.*

- *Breathe deeply three times. Join middle finger with thumb.*

- *Enter into contact with your heart.*

- *Invoke the Holy Spirit which is the redemptory Light of God.*

- *It takes the form of the Violet Light. Feel it entering you.*

- *Allow yourself to feel forgiven in its benevolent presence.*

- *When you are ready, bring to mind people that you have to forgive.*

- *Anything pending with your partner, sister, brother, daughter, son, parents, friends.*

- *Visualize the Violet Light coming down from heaven as a curtain of light that envelops you.*

- *Now see those people around you surrounded by a white light.*

- *See now the Violet Light surrounding them.*

- *Go to your heart.*

- *Observe anything that is pending with those persons.*

- *See the Violet Light now purifying it, cleaning the dirty crystal of the heart.*

- *The Violet Light cleans it until it is completely translucent.*

- *Now see clearly a violet flame burning brightly in your heart.*

- *See it also in theirs: a loving violet flame, shinning bright.*

- *Accept for you now the vision of innocence.*

- *See yourself being innocent, you can feel it. Feel their innocence too.*

- *Feel liberated, renewed, light.*

- *Now, feel deep love for yourself and for all of them.*

Come out of meditation when you are ready. Give thanks to the Violet Light as a manifestation of The Holy Spirit. Thank also those people you invoked.

Repeat this exercise as much as you wish.

•

PRINCIPLES OF FORGIVENESS

- To forgive is to retake the power of your freedom.
    - It is to decide to be free.
    - It is not giving your power to another.
    - It is not to be a victim.
    - It is to be bigger than the offence.
    - It is to avoid condemnation.
    - When you condemn your brother, you condemn yourself.
    - To be the judge of your brother only chains you.

- Your mission is to be in peace.
- Through forgiveness, through the connection with the Holy Spirit.
- It is to choose peace.
- Your function is not to judge, it is to be in peace.
- It is necessary to enter into forgiveness because your peace lies in it.

- **Forgiveness = No judgment**
    - Only when you release your judgments you are in peace.
    - But you cannot control your mind...
    - What do you do?
    - Humility: you ask God for help. You invoke the Violet Light.
    - The Violet Light makes God more accessible to you.

- **In order to create peace:**
    - Observe what you are sowing.
    - Are you creating disharmony or peace?
    - What you are sowing now to satisfy your desire of revenge, later it will be your harvest. So reflect before you act.
    - If all would do actions of peace, there would be peace.
    - Begin with yourself.

- Forgiveness is prosperity because you advance.
- Do to others what you want to be done to you = Forgiveness.
- Leave justice to God.
- You have to be in peace and remain in peace through forgiveness.
- Forgiveness purifies you and allows you to see the Truth.
- Enter the realm of: "Forgiving before judging."

Conclusion

As we have seen, you have to purify your heart or there is no peace for you. This purification is what the Violet Light does to your heart. A purified heart sees innocence in oneself and in others. Then we can all move away from a world of guilt, punishment and control. We can then find peace. The Violet Light assists you immensely in achieving all this. Guilt does not clean anything. The only one who can truly purify your heart is God through His Holy Spirit. The Violet Light is an emanation of the Holy Spirit of God.

-

"Put Violet Light in your heart for five minutes.
Feel forgiveness for others and for the world.
See your innocence and that of all."

THE RIGHT PERSPECTIVE

"The global change has to come from above. It cannot come from the human sphere, because the human sphere is so absorbed in the arrogance of its own power, that it still believes that God is not necessary. It still does not understand that the ego has to die.

With God you cannot be half partner – "you and I," "you God do your share and I will do mine." What has to be undergone is a true surrender to Him, to His superior Will – Love: the renouncement of the ego.

This global change of consciousness thus, comes from the higher spiritual sphere in order to take the human being out of the madness in which he lives – its own inner misery – the ignorance of his own identity and of the purpose of his life and God.

It is the light of the Holy Spirit entering the heart of Man, that changes his vision for one of love and peace, redeemed by the liberating force of the Holy Spirit. It is the vision of peace."

— K a h a n

OFFERING ALL TO GOD

As we offer all to God, everything is resolved because we are invoking the power that can solve it. As we retain our conflicts and our issues, we literally keep them. To invoke the Grace of God for the resolution of all our situations, is to inject light into them and to take them to the sphere where they can truly be resolved. In this meditation we offer all to God, even the good things, because in that we ask the energy of His Grace to empower them.

- *Enter into a quiet space inside yourself. Breathe deeply*
- *Place your hands above your knees, palms facing heaven*
- *See the Violet Light surrounding you and entering your heart*
- *Know that the Violet Light is the presence of God*
- *Speak to it in your heart:*
- *I surrender my pain to the Violet Light*
- *I surrender my worries to the Light*
- *I surrender my anxiety to the Light*
- *I surrender my tension to the Light*
- *I surrender my fear to the Light*
- *I surrender my weakness to the Light*
- *I surrender my addictions to the Light*
- *I surrender my needs to the Light*
- *I surrender my loneliness to the Light*
- *I surrender my limitations to the Light*
- *I surrender my love to the Light*
- *I surrender my happiness to the Light*
- *I surrender my expectations to the Light*
- *I surrender my objectives to the Light*
- *I surrender my life to the Light...*

You can create your own list.

Practice this any time you need to free yourself from a contracting situation. Any time life does not flow... and any time you are well.

– CHAPTER 10 –

•

THE VIOLET LIGHT ACTIVATION
YOUR DIRECT CONNECTION TO UNIVERSAL POWER

"There is nothing more powerful
than the Holy Spirit."
– Kahan

The Violet Light is an emanation of the Holy Spirit: "Grace," "Shekinah," "Shakti," whatever spiritual name you want to give it. The Activation is a descent of The Holy Spirit. You now are going to receive this connection. The Masters and I want it to happen for you, so you have all the support of our will which manifests it.

We now enter the key part of this teaching: the most direct contact with the energy of the Violet Light. Follow step by step without hurry. Be serene, collected, silent.

This is a powerful spiritual experience. I will guide you through it. Allow yourself time for this. You need to enter slowly and come out slowly. After it, you should go out into an open natural space and stay there for a while. So allow yourself at least an hour for the two meditations, and then at least half an hour to an hour to be outside.

This activation is a spiritual initiation: your energy and your awareness will be changed, expanded, elevated The activation is an extremely positive change, most probably you have been waiting for in your life. This first meditation on your chakras will prepare you to receive the activation of the Violet Light, immediately after. The chakras are energy centers that support your life. They are in your aura and correspond to areas of your body.

The next meditation prepares the chakras energetically, stabilizing them, opening them and allowing the spiritual energy to flow correctly. This is what the Golden Light does to them.

This is a sacred moment for you. It starts here...

ACTIVATION OF THE CHAKRAS

Surround yourself with a mystical atmosphere in a quiet place in your home. Switch off or dim the light, you can light a candle and an incense stick. Put soft relaxing music as background if it helps you. Switch off all the phones. Sit on a cushion comfortably with crossed legs by the candle. If you can't, sit on a chair.

We enter into meditation...

♦   *Put your hands on your knees facing up.*

♦   *Breathe deeply three times as you close your eyes, then open them again to read.*

♦   *Now join your middle finger with the thumb in each hand.*

♦   *Visualize a ray of Golden Light that reaches you from heaven and enters you through the Crown Chakra – at the top of your head. Close your eyes to do this.*

♦   *This Golden Divine Light goes down through you to reach the First Chakra: at the base of your column. Just focus on the base of your spine.*

♦ *Concentrate there and visualize the Golden Light in the form of a ball of Light – the size of a tennis ball – filling this area of your spine completely, with all the energy and consciousness of the Golden Light.*

♦ *Close your eyes and stay with that vision for about five minutes. If you know where all the chakras are, remain with your eyes closed, and concentrate on each chakra for about five minutes each, seeing in each one the ball of Golden Light. Moving from the lowest to the highest.*

♦ *If you don't know them, read or memorize their position from below.*

♦ *Do the same with each chakra. Visualize the ball of Golden Light for a few minutes in 2nd Chakra: two inches below the navel; 3rdChakra: solar plexus; 4th Chakra: heart chakra in the center of your chest; 5th Chakra: in the throat; 6th Chakra: third eye, the middle of your forehead; 7th Chakra:- The "Sahasrara" – the crown of your head.*

♦ *Stay with each one for a few minutes.*

When you finish, breathe deeply and slowly three times. Become aware of your body, your surroundings…the here and now.

Remain silent for we continue…

VIOLET LIGHT ACTIVATION

This activation is for you and all. As you receive it, it also expands to all of humanity and the planet.

If the incense has burnt out, you may want to light another one. Observe the inner state the Golden Light has given you.

Leave any worries aside you are in the best hands. God is with you very intensely right now. The spiritual Masters responsible for the Violet Light and for your evolution are also with you guiding, supervising the process.

For the reference color to visualize, you can use the color of the cover or back cover of the book. It is a deep amethyst color. If you cannot visualize it, DO NOT WORRY. The important thing is to focus on the light as it is mentioned.

But... have in mind that you are only focusing your mind as you are guided. The Violet Light will be there whether you do it "right" or not. So relax success does not depend on you.

Remember not to be obsessed by details. I take you through the process with the instructions, but what matters is the experience, the connection, not the words.

The instructions you read are keys to set the process in motion. Read them intently with attention and slowly. Give yourself some time to feel each step. Make an inner decision to open up completely to receive this Grace of God. Feel that you really want to connect with the Violet Light with all your heart.

Jesus said:
"When you let all fear go, a great love will enter you."

Allow the Divine Love in the form of the Violet Light to enter into you completely.

Phase I

♦   *Breathe deeply three times.*

♦   *Put together your middle finger and thumb of each hand. This is the "mudra" of compassion.*

♦   *Read this invocation aloud to activate completely the energy at this moment – Speak out serenely from your heart:*

"I INVOKE GOD AS THE POWER SOURCE OF ALL LIFE, I INVOKE THE VIOLET LIGHT AS AN EMANATION OF GRACE OF THAT UNIVERSAL SOURCE, I INVOKE ALL THE BEINGS OF LIGHT, ALL ASCENDED MASTERS, THE "I AM" PRESENCE OF MY LUMINOUS HIGHER SELF AND THE ARCHANGELS AND ANGELS THAT SUPPORT THE WORK OF THE VIOLET LIGHT, TO BE HERE WITH ME AND ALL TO TAKE US ALL TO THE HIGHEST, AS THEY INITIATE US IN THE VIOLET LIGHT AND ITS GRACE, SO THAT WE ARE TAKEN TO THE SPIRITUAL KINGDOMS OF THE DIVINE FATHER SOURCE WHERE THE VIOLET LIGHT DWELLS. THANK YOU."
AMEN.

♦   *Let the natural rhythm of your breathing take you inside.*

♦   *Allow your inner state of serenity be your support – give yourself to it.*

Phase II

♦   *Visualize yourself completely surrounded by a bright White Light for 2 minutes. Close your eyes now and after each instruction.*

♦   *See the White Light becoming a Gold Light. 2 minutes.*

♦   *Visualize how the Gold Light becomes intense Violet Light and surrounds you completely. 2 minutes.*

◆ *Now, visualize the Violet Light descending upon you from the spiritual planes of God Source.*

◆ *The Violet Light enters you through the Crown Chakra and surrounds your aura with Violet Light.*

Physical body

◆ *Now the Violet Light fills your physical body completely, impregnating all your physical structures with Violet Light: bones – muscles – organs – nervous system – blood – skin – hair. See how the Violet Light is absorbed into your body from the cells to its totality. Now your body starts to vibrate completely in the frequency of the Violet Light. Stay there for 3-5 minutes. Eyes closed.*

Emotional field

◆ *The Violet Light now fills your emotional field. See the first four inches – ten centimeters – of your aura filled with Violet Light.*

◆ *All your feelings and emotions become impregnated now with the vibration and consciousness of the Violet Light, filling your entire emotional field with the energy and vibration of the Violet Light. 3-5 minutes. Eyes closed.*

Mental field

◆ *See now how the Violet Light fills your mental field, the following four inches – ten centimeters – of your aura.*

◆ *See all your thoughts and ideas impregnated with the energy of the Violet Light, filling the totality of your mental field with the consciousness and vibration of the Violet Light. 3-5 minutes. Eyes closed.*

Spiritual field

♦ *Visualize how the Violet Light fills completely your spiritual field, the next three feet of your aura or more, – one meter – impregnating all the space of your Higher Spiritual Nature with the vibration and consciousness of the Violet Light. 5 minutes. Eyes closed.*

Phase III
Chakras

♦ *Visualize now how the Violet Light reaches your first chakra at the bottom of your spine, and fills this chakra completely impregnating it with the vibration and consciousness of the Violet Light.*

♦ *See the chakra as a circle or a ball full of Violet Light.*

♦ *Allow about three minutes for each.*

♦ *Do the same with each chakra. Visualize the ball of Violet Light for a few minutes each in 2nd Chakra: 2 inches below the navel; 3rd Chakra: solar plexus; 4th Chakra: heart chakra in the center of your chest; 5th Chakra: in the throat; 6th Chakra: third eye, the middle of your forehead; 7th Chakra: the "Sahasrara" – the crown of your head, see them all full of Violet Light. Stay there for 10 minutes.*

♦ *Now feel the energy of the Violet Platinum Light – a very bright and luminous Violet Light – surrounding you completely. Allow its love in you to be your support. Let it take you completely into your Inner Self. Feel it in the center of your heart a bright flame, and above your head as a point of Violet Light. Stay there for a while.*

♦ *Before coming out, surround yourself with an aura of brilliant white light for one minute or more.*

When you feel ready, come out breathing deeply three times, and slowly become aware of your physical body, surroundings...the here and now.

Open your eyes. Remain silent and stay where you are for a few minutes. Focus your eyes on a fixed point before you – you can use the lit tip of the incense, if still burning – and allow all the inner state you have, to come out and surround you. When you are ready, move naturally.

Before anything else, give thanks to God Source, to the Violet Light, to all the beings of light, all Ascended Masters, Archangels of light and angels, as well as to the Presence of your Luminous Self for the Activation you have received. Offer with love the Light and Grace present in the Activation, so that they also reach all humanity and the planet for the blessing and freedom of all.

The Violet Light radiates now from you. Now you and your life are supported by the consciousness and energy of the Violet Light.

Now you can take a break.
Go out to an open space, a park, the beach. Walk and feel the Universe and God with you.

As you feel in touch with everything, let your energy and aura feel expanded to all that natural space.

•

AFTER THE ACTIVATION

This is not the end of the activation. The energy will be quite strong for many days. And it is active in you for the rest of this life and beyond. Make sure you drink plenty of water for four days.

ABOUT THE COLORS

Violet

The color that can appear inside your meditation can be soft or deep violet. It does not matter what color appeared inside you. If none appeared, it is not important. The energy is there and you sure felt it. If you did not, have patience. Your aura needs to be purified, refined before you start feeling the energy. It was there. It is always there. When you enter into meditation you can aim at visualizing mainly deep violet, the rich color of most amethysts. This is the way to go in. It can happen that you may not visualize the color in your mind. Do not be concerned about this. The energy will be invoked anyway. As you get practice trying to "see" the color in your mind, it will start to become clear for you. You can practice this by looking at the cover of the book, or at an amethyst stone for a minute. Then close your eyes and try to see the color in your mind. This is just a help for your concentration. The vision of the Violet Light is something different. It will appear to you inside when you less expect it.

Violet Platinum

Platinum is one of the latest frequencies that have been incorporated to this work of the Violet Light. Platinum Light is a very bright white/silver energy. It is now one of the frequencies of the Violet Light. It adds luminosity to the Violet Light when it merges with it.

This shows as an iridescent Violet Light. It can be very bright and it might appear to you at some point.

These are the references. If you cannot visualize them, do not worry. The energy is there. The important thing is to feel it. Just follow the instructions and put your intention into it without worry, and it will all flow naturally at the right time.

WATERING THE SEEDS OF LIGHT

What you have received is a powerful seed of spiritual development and self-realization. This spark of light can, and must be intensified through your loving attention and careful work. The way to do it is meditation. Daily meditation will increase your connection with the Violet Light and with your inner Luminous Self. This will anchor the energy of the light to you and move you and your life forward. Constancy and patience are key here. With your loving dedication to meditation, you will make of this seed a wonderful forest. Although powerful and unlimited, this activation is like the tip of the iceberg: much more lies hidden under it.

Your challenge is to uncover the gold mine of infinite bliss and Grace the Violet Light holds inside, as you expand this birth into its full maturity and fruition. You cannot imagine from this standpoint what lies ahead, for you still haven't seen the energy in action. This is like a scratch on the surface of an inner universe full of wonders. There is an unknown freedom waiting for you product of the immense love power held in the Violet Light.

To get there as from today, meditate in any or all of the following ways.

VIOLET LIGHT DAILY MEDITATIONS

I.

♦ *In your place of meditation, create the sacred atmosphere: candle, incense.*

♦ *Sit down, back straight without tension, fingers middle and thumb touching.*

♦ *Close your eyes.*

♦ *Breathe deeply three times.*

♦ *See yourself surrounded by a bright White Light. One or two minutes.*

♦ *See how this light becomes a beautiful Golden Light that surrounds you as an aura. One minute.*

♦ *Visualize the Golden Light turning into a deep Violet Light that surrounds you completely.*

♦ *Stay in the Violet Light for as long as you want. Minimum 20 minutes.*

♦ *If you feel you want more:*

♦ *Surround yourself with the Platinum Violet Light.*

♦ *Come out by breathing deeply three times. Become aware of your body, your surroundings. Give thanks.*

II.

♦ *The same atmosphere and posture.*

♦ *Visualize a Ray of Violet Light coming down from the Divine Source and entering your Crown Chakra. Then feel this light coming down and entering your heart. Now the Violet Light* fills you with it from the heart, and it also surrounds your aura with Violet Light. Try turning this light into a more Violet Platinum Light.

♦ *Stay there for at least 20 min.*

♦ *Come out by breathing deeply three times. Become aware of your body, your surroundings. Give thanks.*

III.

♦ *The same preparation.*

♦ *See the Violet Light being generated from the center of your heart.*

♦ *See how it expands from the heart to all your being.*

♦ *Feel it expanding beyond yourself to the world and the Universe. Stay in meditation for twenty minutes.*

♦ *Come out by breathing deeply three times. Become aware of your body, your surroundings. Give thanks.*

You can join the third meditation with the second, if you wish.

Surround yourself with brilliant white light for a minute before coming out of the meditations. You can use the Violet Platinum Light in any of these meditations. You may choose one of them or the three any time. If you do two or the three at once, you do not need to do 20 minutes with each. Divide your meditation time into the different parts.

●

LUMINOUS SELF MEDITATON

This is a very powerful meditation you can do any time. It is a direct contact with your Luminous Self. It activates its consciousness in you. The Luminous Self is mainly situated above your head like a hovering presence of light. It actually looks like a point of brilliant light. Enough magnetism has to be generated to attract all the goodness of this source of your light, so that it distills its light and bliss on you. This is achieved by generating love for it and going to its encounter in meditation.

- *Create the sacred atmosphere: candle, incense.*

- *Sit down, back straight without tension. Fingers, middle and thumb touching.*

- *Breathe naturally into your solar plexus.*

- *Surround yourself with the Violet Light.*

- *When you breathe in, place your concentration on the top of your head.*

- *Close your eyes after each instruction, and feel for a few minutes.*

- *Now, feel as if you are breathing in the air towards the top of your head. Feel the energy expanding beyond your head upwards.*

- *See the point of bright white light hovering above your head, your Luminous Self. See yourself going up to it through a beam of Platinum Light, that connects the top of your head with the point of light.*

- *Merge with the Luminous Self.*

- *Feel the joy of it bathing your body, your entire self.*

♦ *Feel you are immersed in an ocean of joy made of Violet Light.*

♦ *Bring the consciousness down from the point of light into your head, and then down to the heart. Feel the experience.*

♦ *Go up again from the heart to the top of your head, to the point of light. Stay there for some minutes.*

♦ *Before coming out, let all the energy from the point of light fall on you and center yourself in the heart.*

♦ *Breathe deeply three times. Become aware of your body, of your surroundings. Come out of the meditation. Give thanks to the light, to your Luminous Self.*

MEDITATION TIME

To make the most of the meditation do two sessions a day:
- One as you wake up
- The other before going to bed

This will allow you to still your mind as you connect with your inner self, before you engage in the affairs of the world, in the mornings, and at night, you touch again the eternal in you through the Violet Light, once you have finished all mundane activities. Your progress this way is much faster and firm. You might find that something moves inside you – changes in perspective, in attitude. Be grateful every day for this and for what you have been given, and you will be opening up for more. Try to do a minimum of fifteen to twenty minutes in each meditation. Beyond this you can stay an hour or two if you want.

IMPORTANT ADVICE

I.

It is very important that you keep a practice of meditation daily, if you want to get the most out of this. It is your decision. You have to see what your personal, spiritual goals are. What quality of inner connection you wish to experience.

The Violet Light dissolves most old crystallizations easily. But the mind is structured, so the footprints often remain on it when an old structure goes. The mind's tendency is to act as if it was still there, and it will fill that space with thought energy, as if nothing has happened. To avoid that you need to still the mind more and more through meditation. Then the space left by the pattern, will be filled with light and consciousness. The Violet Light has an immense power to free you. Your job is to make sure your mind does not recreate those patterns, which have been dissolved by the light. What remains in the mind is like a memory of the pattern. Do not fall for the memory of it. The crystallized pattern is gone. But the thoughts about it often remain: the footprints. Become strong in contact with the light. Fill the spaces left, with light and love.

II.

Take into account that you are not immune to negative ego and its reactions, unless you are exposed to the divine energy source in meditation enough. I have seen this too often: people with great spiritual activation becoming easy prey for negative ego. The unmistakable sign that there is not enough exposure to higher frequencies of light: not enough meditation. It is common for the lazy mind to think that everything is done for it. It takes a course or receives an initiation and thinks that is it. Then people tend to meditate now and again thinking the work is being done. Do not make the same mistake: it is not. The pull of the ego downwards is very strong; the pull of the world towards keeping the same obsolete patterns in you, is stronger and if one is not deeply rooted in the inner truth and has a clear inner vision, one ends up thinking one is very enlightened but behaves like a reckless ignorant.

Remember that you acquire the consciousness and energy of what you are exposed to, and that is what you will repeat in your life. If there is not enough exposure to the purity and elevation of the inner divine energy, you are spending most of your time in contact with the lower frequencies of the ego and the world. They will rule you and rule your life. Enough exposure is daily exposure, if not it is like trying to keep a garden beautiful but doing a little one day, then some more two weeks later; it never gets anywhere. So if you want things to work for the best getting all the power from this energy, keep exposing yourself to it. Think how many years in your life and how much time each day, you have been and are still exposed to lower vibrations. It takes a lot of work to curve the tendency of the mind and of the ego, on the way to true freedom, and doing it only for a few months won't get the job done. Many lose their inertia after a while, thinking they got good results, they feel better so they stop. Then they start sliding down, because they did not get far enough to be able to keep up there. Remember that. You, like most, have been exposed to lower vibrations for many years, so don't expect that the negative tendencies they bring, will be completely reversed in a few months.

The moment you stop meditating ego increases and consciousness decreases. If you meditate, ego decreases and consciousness increases. This will be true until you have reached such inner firmness, that negative ego has no effect on you whether you meditate or not. That takes a while. If you keep doing it, it will get better and better every day. Even after you have reached that point of stability and firmness, you will want to keep meditating for the sheer bliss of it.

If you are serious about changing and about becoming truly loving, really happy and prosperous, get serious about the work. This light is one of the most powerful tools you will find on this planet to move you and your life forward. But you have to do your part of the work. If you already expose yourself to meditation or to divine energy from your own spiritual practice, the principles for you are the same. I invite you to surround your practice with the Violet Light and to see what it does for you. You might find a great surprise as I did when I put Violet Light into my original spiritual practices: the effects doubled.

This is the first part of the Activation. There are two other parts further on to complete your activation. Keep reading. Remember daily, that the presence of God in the form of the Violet Light is with you to support you.

●

"For a few minutes surround your intimate partner or dearest person with Violet Light."

– CHAPTER 11 –

•

THE DOORS TO ALL YOUR SECRETS: THE CHAKRAS

*"We need something that opens
our heart, so we really see what
it feels like to be there."*
– Kahan

These famous wheels of energy make up the centers of the principal energy system in the Human Being. Chakra means "wheel" and as a wheel, they turn. They do not go anywhere, but allow energy to do so as it goes through them. They are situated in different parts of your aura and relate to specific areas of the body, as we have seen in the Activation. They are responsible for the different areas of your consciousness. What is relevant here is that a proper functioning of the chakras cannot be taken for granted, and this is where the issue really starts.

Since they can be open, closed or partially open energy will flow or will be blocked in them. So your consciousness in the area of the chakra will be lacking or it will manifest. A closed chakra blocks light, making that area of your consciousness contracted. As my aura-reading friend from Mexico would say, karmas reside in them, blocking their capability of energy flow, as dry leaves would block the drain of a courtyard on a rainy autumn day.

There has to be a solution to this. A chakra blocked by Karma, is a chakra that attracts to you like a magnet a specific karma from the world outside. The Violet Light has an effect on each chakra deactivating the power of the magnet, dissolving your karmas thus opening the chakra to its complete functioning and to all its spiritual power. This nonetheless takes time and effort. Be sure that an acceleration in the liberation of the chakras is taking place, as the Violet Light enters them. Then it depends on your constancy with meditation, and in maintaining the new correct attitudes developed by the Light in you, until they become solid. Impeccability with your energy will do the rest, making sure you steer away from rocky waters: low vibrations.

The reason I have put the Activation before the chakras, is to avoid your mind thinking about the content of each chakra as the meditation process was taking you through them. The best way to enter into the Activation is with an empty mind.

THE SEVEN CHAKRAS
The effect of the Violet Light on each chakra

> *"As the higher vibration of light touches you, you develop and advance."*

1.- Survival energy: Impulse of life

Situated at the base of the spine, this chakra connects with the energy of survival. This manifests as the instinct for survival and its related sexual energy. Applying Violet Light to this chakra allows the sexual energy to be raised to the other chakras. This allows the use of the energy for other purposes. The true meaning of sexual energy is that of survival, survival of life and continuing of the species. Therefore in this chakra lies the consciousness of surviving. The Violet Light in it, also eliminates and transmutes the anxiety of survival we all have, integrating a deep sense of peace to mind and body, as it connects us with our eternal awareness that, as soul energy, there is no death for us therefore no anxiety about surviving.

2.- Vital energy – "Chi"

This chakra, two inches below the navel, is an important center of vital energy we call "Chi" – the "Prana" of the Hindu tradition. The Violet Light here stills the Chi giving the person vitality and energy accumulated as a reserve. Stilling the Chi is fundamental, for it means stilling the energy in the body and calming the mind. Human beings have very agitated Chi because their minds are agitated. This chakra activated by the Violet Light, also gives depth, rooting and stability since it is a chakra related to the element earth, "connection with the earth." It also confers strength of life, healing – energetic regeneration – and a more intuitive connection with life. When properly opened it activates sensation awareness and intuitive knowledge, moving you beyond the need of having to analyze or think everything. It means to be in touch with the earth energy and the wise energies of the body.

3.- Ego

This chakra is the seat of the ego and it is situated in the solar plexus. Here the Violet Light produces the transmutation of the ego, liberating fears, guilt, anger, thus softening the ego. It liberates the sense of the small "I" and "mine," freeing us from the terrible clutch of their limiting influence. Then we can enter fully into the new consciousness of "together" and "ours." This produces a relaxation of this area of our consciousness, as it becomes expanded having been freed from those negative emotions. In this expansion we find greater energy and a better flow of it, increasing our ability to be in touch with life and others, as well as with ourselves, since the contractions fear produced kept us in an energetic separation from life. So properly opened and functioning, we are expanded from here to a connection with our whole being and the whole of life. As this happens, we transcend the ego. In transcending the ego one can rise to the consciousness of the fourth chakra.

4.- Love

Situated in the center of the chest at the level of the heart. Jung said that here the cosmic man is born. When the consciousness is liberated from the claws of the ego in the third chakra, it can access love fully in the fourth. The Violet Light produces that elevation through the transmutation of the third and the opening of the fourth. When consciousness or energy has been liberated from the other three chakras, we can talk of a true experience of unconditional love in the fourth chakra. The Violet Light transmutes here the concept of "my love" into Universal Love. It also opens it to the experience of generosity, forgiveness, acceptance, tolerance and compassion. God in action = Love.

5.- Communication

Situated in the throat, this chakra controls our communication. The Violet Light frees here communication problems. It produces openness. Here lies the power of mantra through words charged with the high vibration of the Violet Light. So we learn here to speak truth and love. Generally the Violet Light in this chakra brings the liberation of emotions that have not been expressed – repressed or forgotten. It moves the individual to talk his or her highest truth. It also confers the power to know when to be silent. This is a door that has two directions: giving – expression; receiving – silence. The wisdom to give and to receive: mutual exchange. It also produces a connection of the inner and the superior aspects of the person, with the external aspects. If there is a correct alignment with the previous chakra, what we are going to communicate here is Love.

6.- Vision

Right in the forehead, this so called "third eye" is considered the eye that "sees." For the other two, seeing duality, do no see at all. Truth must be seen as a single reality away from a dual world that is, in its nature, deceitful. One single eye therefore would see unity when opened, and this is what you start to see when the Violet Light touches this chakra. We also have here the vision of the Inner Self as inner light, and of inner subtle worlds belonging to the realm of Spirit. Something the other two eyes do not see. The Violet Light provides here clarity. If you put the Light in this chakra, you can illuminate your mind and have true vision and therefore understanding. You can clarify an issue by putting the Light in this chakra. Since the Violet Light transmutes the sense of the ephemeral, it is going to give us a vision of the permanent clearer, stronger and closer. The inner vision this chakra manifests when fully active, is the vision of the Self from the Self.

7.- Spiritual Realization

Peace is the key word here. Situated at the top of the head the "Crown" chakra is truly the top of our consciousness. The Violet Light upon touching this area of our consciousness will truly increase it, expanding our spirituality, providing peace, wisdom and serenity. Through the creation of a strong connection with God, faith is restored and strengthened. This is what happens when the Violet Light touches this chakra. It implies the development of a very high understanding, the highest: Spiritual Enlightenment. By it everything is seen and experienced as caused by, and infused with Spirit. It also brings knowledge of God as an experience of the Divine, a great experience of love otherwise unknown to Man, a love that permeates everything filling you with an ecstatic joy. In this knowledge of God the mysteries of the Universe are revealed. Fusion with God as One is the knowledge that "I Am God." This is the death of the individual ego-consciousness. The rebirth of our Universal Consciousness.

THE CHAKRA SYSTEM:
A MAP OF YOURSELF

This chakra system becomes a complete map of yourself. A perfect guide by which to identify area problems, and with the powerful help of the Violet Light, to become really free of them. If you need to work with more than one healing, you can do them together reducing the global time or do them separate at your discretion.

CHAKRA HEALINGS

These healings will be much more powerful and effective, if you have done the activation of the Violet Light in the book. They all have to do with increasing the light in an area of yourself. I describe the action to take in the healing section of each case, without pause. When you actually do it, make sure you allow some moments or minutes between each instruction of the healing; in this way you can experience every step and can get into all the benefits. Let your intuition guide you through what feels right for you. We will address some of the most common situations.

Communication problems

The problem
If you do not express your emotions and keep them inside, you need to transmute this blockage and allow your emotions to flow. In that self-expression, you will find power and creativity, as well as togetherness.

The healing
Bring Violet Light to your throat chakra. In meditation, concentrate on your fifth chakra, on the throat, visualizing the Violet Light there. See the chakra as a circle a little smaller than a compact disk, and see that circle filled with Violet Light, that comes from your heart or from

above you. Do this every day for ten minutes until you feel a positive change in you.

Overactive mind – worrying

The problem
An issue is in your mind and it is going around taking your peace away. The issue is not resolving itself. You have a worrying attitude about something in your life. You do not know what to do. It is keeping you tensed, stressed, you can't sleep well. You need to calm your mind and see clearly, so that you can act promptly in the right direction.

The healing
Sit down. Breathe deeply three times, following the air in and out with your attention. See the Violet Light coming down on you; it enters your forehead, 6th chakra. See it intensely filled with Violet Light, like a bright star. Bring all that light down to the heart chakra, the 4th. See the star from the forehead merge into the heart. The star becomes now a sun of Violet Light. Then it turns into a sun of Golden Light. Do it for three days or more for ten minutes.

Developing love

The problem
You are not loving or merciful. You are a rigid character that suffer because cannot be soft, tender, loving. You want everything to be right and therefore are not tolerant with others or with yourself. You cannot relate to close ones in a warm manner. And you do not expose your feelings. You are too concerned about being hurt. You would like things to be different; this situation makes you unhappy. You long for the opening of your heart so that you can be warm and loving, in the pursuit of your inner and outer happiness. As you put love into life, life will bring you love.

The healing
Visualize Violet Light coming from above and entering into your head, then feel it going into your heart. See the Violet Light concentrating on the heart. It takes the form of an intense light. Feel the sweetness of the light and let it fill your heart, let it fill you with it. See a violet flame in the center of your heart. Forgive, in this state. Let go. Forgive yourself. Understand yourself and allow yourself to be free from this condition. You deserve peace, love. Receive them now. Feel love and gratitude for yourself. Do this every day for ten minutes or more until you feel a great improvement.

Fear

The problem
You have fearful reactions to life situations and to people. This withdraws you from life and from others. You stop doing things because of fear. You need to develop a confident attitude to life, in which you expect positive outcomes and enjoy working for them, as well as receiving them. You will then feel you deserve the best for you. You deserve to be alive and to feel free to be yourself fully.

The healing
Sit down in silence. Breathe deeply six times. Feel safe. See the Violet Light embracing you. It filters into your aura, body, bones. It relaxes you. Feel the safety there. Understand this is the truth: your state of calm, love and peace. Observe your breathing, free, relaxed... it is only your mind creating fear. See the Violet Light now entering into your mind from above, filling all the corners of it; your mind is filled with the light. See the areas of your life that produce fear in you. Picture them in your mind and see yourself in them. Put Violet Light into those areas and into you in them. Now put Violet Light in the 3rd chakra: solar plexus; in the 4th chakra: heart area; and in the 5th chakra: throat. Do this every day for at least 15 minutes, for a month.

Living with doubts

The problem
You are unsure about things. You have doubts about everything. You have doubts about yourself. You do not have faith in you or in life. You need to connect with your center from where you will feel strength and faith to be and act.

The healing
Stand up. Close your eyes. See a beam of Violet Light coming down on you from heaven. It goes right through you very intensely and anchors itself into the ground. Feel you are wired to this beam of light. Feel it pulsating, buzzing with energy inside you as you become strengthened from the inside out. Stay like this for five minutes. Now concentrate on the 7th chakra – top of your head – and see there the Violet Light as a ray of light that comes to you from God. Feel you are faith. Feel you are connected with God and with the Universe. Do it daily for as long as necessary.

Confusion

The problem
You live very confused. You do not know what to do or where to go. You are not sure what is best or what is real in life for you. You need to unload your mind to have clarity, feel your heart and follow it without interferences.

The healing
Focus the Violet Light on your 6th chakra – forehead. Keep it there intensely for ten minutes. See how the light enters into the chakra and opens it like a beautiful flower, filling your inner mind with Violet Light. Do this every day for ten minutes for some weeks.

Negative emotions

The problem
You are reacting emotionally to life. You find anger, guilt, fear, frustration and other emotions limit your experience of a peaceful happy life. You need to move away from taking things personally; nobody is after you. You need to feel life supports you.

The healing
Visualize Violet Light on your 3rd chakra – solar plexus. See the Light going really into it and expanding the chakra. Feel a great space in that area. See it as a circle of Violet Light that becomes expanded like a sun. After a while, take all that light to the 4th chakra, in the center of the chest. Stay in it seeing the Violet Light there, and feel your heart expanding. Do this for ten minutes twice every day until you feel a real change.

A BRIEF GUIDE

You can put Violet Light in the following chakras for five to ten minutes a day:

- Develop love or expansion – go to chakras 3rd & 4th

- Increase your spirituality, inner peace, love: 7th & 4th

- Increase your energy: 1st 2nd & 3rd

- Activate your intuition: 2nd & 6th

- Free your communication: 5th

- Enhance your connection with life: 3rd

- Liberation of fears: 3rd

- Calm your mind: 3rd and 6th

– CHAPTER 12 –

•

ACTIVATION – PART II: INTEGRATING THE LIGHT IN YOU

"Truth is a proof of love."
– Kahan

This part of the Activation is to intensify the high level of vibration of the Violet Light in you, and to deeply connect the Violet and Gold Light to your body and aura. The Gold Light is united to the Violet Light. They are really the same. To our mind that seems strange, but the realm of spirit cannot be understood with the limitations of the mind and its lineal processes.

The Gold Light and the Violet Light are like the two sides of a coin. They tend to superimpose on each other. I often joke with the people in the course. They often see Violet Light in the meditation of the Golden Light we did with you before. Then I ask them how that happened, when we were only doing Gold light not Violet. Then, when we meditate in this second part of the Activation, or at any other time of the course, they see both Violet and Gold Light. Many people have explained having seen them alternating, for moments they see one, then the other appears. Some have seen Gold Light surrounded with Violet Light or the other way around. A lady once saw a circle of light that was turning around itself. It showed Violet Light on one side and Gold Light on the other. The important thing to understand is that the Violet Light takes us to the Golden state of spirituality. The vibration of the Violet Light generates Gold Light. Then the Gold Light emanates the high spiritual frequencies of the Violet Light. They are the two colors of the highest spiritual state. One generates the other in an ascending spiral of increasing vibration.

•

Now we enter into the activation meditation:

- *The preparation and posture are the same as in the first part of the Activation.*

- *Sitting down with fingers in the mudra of compassion: middle finger joining the thumb.*

- *Breathe deeply three times.*

- *Visualize Gold Light descending on you from the highest spiritual planes. Reaching your crown chakra.*

- *This Golden Light is spilled over you like liquid gold.*

- *This golden liquid light covers slowly all your body, moving down like a dense golden liquid. 5 minutes.*

- *Your body becomes a body of Golden Light.*

- *Your aura is made of Gold Light. Stay in this vision for 5 more minutes.*

- *Now see the Violet Light descending from the highest divine plane, and falling on you as it becomes anchored to your body of Gold Light.*

- *See the Violet Light surrounding the Gold Light of your body. It also enters through the Sahasrara – the top chakra – filling your body inside. See the Violet Light surrounding you outside…*

- *…transmuting your aura into the violet color of this celestial light.*

- *Now feel its state and become its consciousness. Merge with it.*

- *Feel that every moment… you are going deeper and deeper into the universe of Violet Light inside of you… feel that more and more every moment... feel merging into the Ocean of Violet Light.*

- *Stay like this for 20 minutes.*

- *Before coming out, surround yourself with a dense, like milk, white light. Do it for a minute or so.*

- *Breathe deeply three times. Become aware of your body, surroundings, sounds.*

- *Give thanks to the Violet Light, to God Source and to the Masters of light.*

When you are ready, come out slowly breathing deeply a couple of times. This is also a very deep and powerful meditation.

Take it easy as you come out or engage in more worldly things. You should take at least half hour. Avoid rushing into things and getting involved.

Spend some time enjoying the peaceful state the meditation has given you. Do not busy yourself straight away. Allow the experience to sink in. embrace the inner state it has given you.

– CHAPTER 13 –

•

PRACTICES:
HOW TO CHANGE YOUR LIFE
AND THE WORLD

*"Good intentions plus true work
in the right direction, with the
correct divine assistance, will
take us all to heaven."*
– Kahan

How to transform all areas of your life, liberate past traumas and long standing emotional conflicts.

The objective of the practices is to take the Violet Light to all areas of your life:
♦   To yourself
♦   To people
♦   To your life situations
♦   To your Meditation
♦   To the World

As far as you are concerned we can talk of:
♦   Help improve your physical, emotional, mental, spiritual areas
♦   Deeply improving: your life, relationships, work, family

About others:
♦   Help ill people
♦   People in crisis
♦   People in the process of dying

Also we will see how to put Violet Light into the past to heal it, into the present to transform it, and how to send Violet Light to someone who needs help or healing. You now vibrate in the frequency of the Violet Light after receiving the Activation. But this is not the end. You can do a great deal to change your life, if you know how. These practices are the channels to use, to put that frequency you now have in your aura to work, in all areas of your life and also in the life of others. They are the keys to open doors to that energy you now have. Through them you can activate all situations with Violet Light, in order to transmute, improve, liberate, elevate, resolve and help. We are going to see how. Remember that miracles happen when you believe in them and work constantly in the right way. You have now one of the best allies: the divine love power of the Violet Light. Let's make it work for the best. It all comes down to going up, to one common mission, one vision which you must never lose: keep your vibration high. This is the key to all practices. What you seek with the use of them all, is keeping your vibration high all the time and never let it come down.

Remember… in high vibration…
♦   You are protected
♦   It liberates you:
o   From fears
o   Darkness
o   Negativity
♦   It reveals the Divine in you
♦   It keeps you in the vibration of light and love
♦   Protected from your own darkness and that of others
♦   You are in love
♦   Your Faith is strong
♦   You express compassion
♦   You live in sweetness
♦   You evolve
♦   You are high
♦   You are with God

•

IMPORTANT REFLECTIONS

The Will of God

In using the practices you are changing the vibration of things, persons, situations. This is what produces the change and the betterment. It is in essence the invocation of the Divine in you and in all. See it in that perspective and you will truly understand the essence of what this is all about. At the end of the day what you are doing is transforming the planet and life upon it. When sending Violet Light to a person or to a situation, you are effectively asking that the Will and the Love of God manifest there: you are giving blessings. So be at peace with it. In praying are you not asking God to change something, to improve, heal or help, in a word to bless you or someone else? It is to ask God to free a person from his or her limitations, in whatever way they are manifesting. The same here. The only difference is the amount of connection with the Grace of God, and the level of God energy which you have available.

To send Violet Light to your brothers is Compassion. To show them the Violet Light is Love. Your Activation reaches them in doing it. To work and put others to work in this manner, is the most real way in which life and this planet can be changed: from within.

Peace Treaties

Peace treaties do not work because they are not signed from a transmuted heart full of forgiveness, tolerance and compassion. Not enough love has been generated in the heart of the ones who sign them or in their peoples' hearts. Intentions are not good enough, they can take us literally to hell, if an inner transformation has not taken place. This is true spiritual work. So, good intentions plus true work in the right direction with the correct divine assistance, will take us all to heaven. The way is to change oneself, and in that power of light that emanates from such a being, that has become an alchemist inside transmuting all his own darkness into light, then we can touch others with our mere presence, and become a catalyst for other people's change and liberation. This is the true path to global peace and harmony, the only real one because this one, does work. From there we can start crystallizing peace treaties with anyone, from our transformed heart in the path to real global peace: an illumined humanity from the illumination of the individual.

PRACTICES: ALL ABOUT THEM

The help given here should not exclude medical or counseling help. This is a system to help improve the life and evolution of the persons involved. It is not intended to replace professional, medical assistance where and when needed.

The idea is that any situation in your life can be improved by putting Violet Light into it. From here everything develops. You can create your own techniques and find new ways and circumstances to which apply the light. You can use the Gold Light to stabilize and strengthen when necessary, when true changes have been accomplished by infusions of Violet Light, or as a preparation before working with the Violet Light. This is your option; use your intuition to know what to do at any time. The Gold Light purifies and brings more light. Use the Golden Light when the acceleration is too much for you. Generally use the Violet Light for everything; it is pure sanctity.

Do not become obsessed by thinking, you must be all day and in all situations sending Violet Light; you won't live. Your aura emanates Violet Light, and this light is radiating to wherever you are, and whoever you are with, will receive it. The practices are to focus the intensity of the Violet Light when required. Also when you want to increase the vibration of a situation, or when you have nothing to do with your mind and instead of thinking idly, you use your mind to send Violet Light.

The way to do it

In all the practices you visualize the Violet Light coming from above and descending upon the person or situation. Other options are to see it coming dawn on you and then coming out of your heart or from your third eye – the forehead chakra. In these cases you visualize a beam of Violet Light coming out of you. By visualizing, you direct the energy from your aura or from heaven. The Violet Light is at your command since you are connected directly with it, through the Activation. Remember that the Light is with you and responds to your higher will.

General Practices

- **Feel parts of your body**, aura, emotions, mind that feel they need healing in you. Put Violet Light into them.

- **Engulf yourself and the situation** you are in, with the light to change a situation at once.

- **If you see someone with problems**, suffering physically or for any other reason, send them the light seeing the Violet Light coming down on them. If it is appropriate, you can show them how to visualize it.

- **Transmute Karmas** you have from the past, from this life or other lives. Just direct Violet Light to them as you picture them in your mind. If they are unknown from other lives, send Violet Light to: "past lives" in your mind. The work will be done.

- **See conflictive situations you have lived** – Recall them with your mind as a movie. See it all happening within the Violet Light: visualize the scenes and everyone in them made of Violet Light.

For this one and others, you can enter into a brief meditation and can work visualizing the situation surrounded with Violet Light.

Daily life practices:

- **See Violet Light in the food you eat**, the water you drink, the water of the shower on you, the air you breathe. You can bless the food with Violet Light putting your hands above it, or with your intention from the heart.

- **In public transport**. This is a good one in which to bathe everyone with Violet Light, since you might be doing nothing, with your mind just waiting to get to your destination.

- **Supermarket**. Visualize all the food and products there surrounded by and filled with Violet Light. You do this generally not one by one, but seeing a full corridor of shelves bathed in Violet Light. You only need to do it in one corridor and from there imagine all are the same. This should take you no more than ten seconds.

- **Place where you live**. You can activate your house with the Violet Light. Stand in the main hall and visualize a ray of Violet Light descending into the center of it, and anchoring itself into the ground. When you see it clearly in your mental vision, expand it in all directions to embrace all the space of the house, until the light surrounds it completely.

- **Workplace.** You can also do this in your place of work.

- **Money** – Turn money into Violet Light: in giving it, when receiving it. See money has an aura of Violet Light.

Any time during the day...

- Visualize an aura of Violet Light surrounding you.

- When with someone, bathe him or her with Violet Light.

- Send Violet Light to close ones.

- Put Violet Light into your life situations: family, work, relationship, knowing that the best will manifest: the Will of God.

Specific situations:

- **Transmutation of pending issues in past relationships**. It is possible to clean them by entering into meditation to create an encounter with that person. As you see inside you the situation with the person, put both of you into an imagined "Violet Fire." Also put the light into the relationship space or the situation between you both. Do it for a while, and when you feel that everything is fine give thanks to the person, who now retires, and you can invoke the next person you have something to work out with. Enter with her into that Violet Fire and do the same. Invoke and ask for the purification of all karmas and pending disharmonious issues, between you both.

- **Solving pending issues with people** – You can also talk with the "double" of a person present in your life, from the past or someone already gone. Convoke him or her to an inner meeting in meditation. Have a dialogue with the person, talk and listen. Do this in an ambience of Violet Light. The point here is to say and hear whatever was never said, and to

137

forgive, being helped by the energy of the Violet Light. At the end hug the person, give thanks to him or her. Let the person go with great respect. Also thank the light and let go of the visualization.

- **Daily encounters** – Whenever you are with someone, you can visualize a beam of Violet Light going from your heart to the heart of that person. Do this in a natural spontaneous way.

All the time you use the Violet Light for something, give thanks to it afterwards.

Decisions

- In any situation in life in which you don't know the right option for you, the path to follow, what choice to make, put Violet Light into all the options and let them go. The most appropriate one will manifest. You must forget about the issue once you have put Violet Light into the options. The best one for you will show up. Maybe none of them will manifest for you. Probably an unexpected one will appear.

Protection

- Seal your aura and your energy with circles of Violet Light around wrists and ankles.

Any time you can say:

"I seal myself completely with the protective power of the Violet Light."

Helping others:

- **Transmute emotional pain** with Violet Light to turn it into acceptance, understanding and love. You can do it to transmute someone's pain or your own pain.

- **If you are a healer,** visualize the Violet Light entering you from above and going out through your hands, to the person you want to help in the session. Visualize Emerald Light, Violet Light and Gold Light surrounding the person as if it was her own aura.

- **Someone in the process of dying** – Send him, her Violet Light. Their process will be better and they will encounter the Violet Light after leaving this plane of existence.

There is a technique that has been developed for this situation, which is very important to take into account:

- Tell the person she is leaving, if she doesn't know. In this way the person can prepare, close her issues and leave in peace.
- Talk to her about God, about the Violet Light.
- Tell her to go to the Light when parting. A light will appear then and he, she will see it.
- If the person is unconscious talk to her anyway.
- She should meditate with the Violet Light if she can, the time before parting, days, weeks.
- Pray for her together.
- Tell her to forgive all and everyone. To release everything, not to hold on to anything. Not to be attached to the things of this world.
- She should let everything go.
- To repent sincerely of anything pending. It is her last opportunity.
- She can put Violet Light in all those things, in karmas or in any resentments.
- She should go very light.

- Tell her to connect with her spiritual guides. To thank them for this life's support.
- To ask them the last favor to guide her with love through to the other side.
- She should not believe she is dying truly. Only the body dies. Not the soul.
- She should keep the Violet Light in the heart, all the time, whatever happens.
- Tell him, her to invoke the Violet Light during the process and when gone.
- She can also invoke, Jesus, the Masters, Saints.
- At the moment of parting, it is very important to think of God or Jesus or Virgin Mary, any spiritual Master or Saint. To think of them or invoke them. Then the person goes to them.
- Also at parting, the person should try to stay conscious connecting with her Higher Self. She should ask the Higher Self to manifest fully and guide the person to the Light.
- After the person has gone, pray for her, ask blessings for her. Also send her Violet Light and Golden Light, see them surrounding her.
- Have no doubt, help arrives to her for her evolution and her peace.

If appropriate, you can teach the person to surround herself with Violet Light and to visualize it in the ill area. You can use all this also for yourself, if necessary.

Connecting with people

- Visualize a Violet Flame in the heart of others blazing brightly. It is an excellent exercise, for you will see the person beyond personality masks and defects, to see the essence of innocence in them. With this, your connection with people will be from the heart and you will help in freeing them from their personality constraints, invoking the awakening of their "Light Self" in the heart.

- You can also see the Violet Light in all hearts, united through rays of this light. And of course, in yours.

Media

- **Newsstand** – When you go past near a newsstand, see it blazing with Violet Fire – to transmute all that is being sold there. Much negativity is produced by the massive printing of "negative news" and its consumption.

- **When hearing news** – radio or seeing TV news, visualize Violet Light around them and a powerful emanation of Violet Light reaching everyone who receives the news.

The Planet

- **You can visualize Violet Light** for the planet and humanity by surrounding them with the light.

- **Group Meditation**. It is an excellent practice for the planet, to get together with a group of friends with the same service attitude. You can gather once a week in a circle of service to meditate for the peace and light of the planet, by sending to it Violet Light all together. You can use the final meditation of the book "Global Meditation" as a good step-by-step planetary meditation.

•

SHARING YOUR LIGHT

As you now have the Violet Light in your aura through the connection with the main source of Violet Light, you have the vibration necessary to impart the light and to ignite flames with your flame. Start lighting violet flames in people's hearts with your love and light. Soon all the world, the whole planet will be lit. Teach people to use and send Violet Light to others who need it and who are suffering. This is pure "Boddhichitta" – pure compassion – using the Buddhist terminology. Everybody becoming a bearer of this flame, all becoming light healers, flames of peace. This is probably one of the most compassionate ways to act: to show your brothers and sisters of humanity, how to heal and change themselves to become free, to enter into peace, to become full of love and true power. Creating beings of consciousness of peace. In a word, it is to help return their Divine Power to them.

There needs to be a lot of transmutation. When you use the Violet Light you will attract the Consciousness and the Will of God. Many things and many people don't let the Will of God manifest in their lives by putting up resistance, putting their non-illuminated will – ego – in the way. In embracing the violet energy, they are going to live the highest life they can live. What can be better than that the inhabitants of the Earth transmute their own planet? Transmutation sometimes is not instant. Sometimes it takes its time, but the application of the Light will accelerate the processes immediately.

"We all deserve to access the Will of God without interference."

UNDERSTANDING FAITH

*"We must leave scientific
explanations to the scientists."*

One key aspect of the work is faith. It is a practical one, for it has to do with the bridge that crosses over the gap between you and Heaven. It is practical because if there is no bridge, how can you make the crossing? To channel water you need the course of a river, that is: a structure, and that structure has to be fit – in working order. To channel energy is the same. Faith is what makes that structure fit for the work, free from weaknesses, from cracks, free from failure. Your body and aura are the structure. Faith makes them strong for the Light to flow through.

Faith and enthusiasm are needed to make it work the best way. Faith is what makes of you a strong vessel – an integrated one that can contain the Divine Grace. If you don't have it, your mental and energetic structure will not be a solid vessel to contain the power. The vessel without faith is a shattered one, and through the cracks energy spills away.

What is faith?

Conviction, certainty. "Conviction in the Divine Power." Jesus was and is pure faith; total conviction in that power of His Father in him. When he speaks to Lazarus, he does not say: "Lazarus… try to see if this thing of getting up works… and if not we will try something else…" He says: "Lazarus, get up and walk." And he does get up and walk. This is what faith is: the decree of total conviction from your divinity. It is doubt what debilitates divine energy.

I designed an equation:
God = Certainty. God ≠ Doubt.

If you doubt, what faith do you have in Him? Power is His.

143

Observe Nature, the manifested power of Creation, there is no doubt in it. The strength of the sea, the rivers, a storm, lightning, a tree, the sun, a birth, fire… there is no doubt in Creation, there is no failure. It is always pushing ahead. Creation never quits. This is faith. One abandons when loosing faith, the conviction, the energy. Enthusiasm comes from faith.

Enthusiasm = energy. Positive attitude.
No enthusiasm = low energy; blockage = fear. It steals energy.
No doubt = firm conviction.

Is there anything in the world that wasn't made with faith? Think about it. Great inventions, a project, a marriage, a career, a house, a home, a child. There is nothing in the world that wasn't made with faith. Faith makes planets move, the Universe exist, you and I act. It is very important to understand the power of faith. If you cannot have faith, feel faith about something, about life and about yourself, be certain there is negativity in you.

Negativity = Denial

So infuse your whole being with the power of faith. Let faith take you high, it can take you very high. Don't resist it with denial. That conviction is the power of God. Everything is aligned with it – it is irresistible. Just put faith in your life and let God do His work. You will be surprised… God is acting. We have an immense power, the power of good through faith. Breathe faith. Violet Light is faith: Violet Faith.

Faith causes

We believe that when something proves that it works, we can have faith in it. The truth is the other way around: faith causes things to work, it causes things into manifestation. So the power is given to us beforehand, by the Spirit of God. Faith is not the effect of a condition. Faith is the cause of that condition. This is the way the Universe works. That is why Jesus said things will be done according to our faith, because faith is the seed of manifestation. I personally have understood many metaphysical laws of life through my work with the Violet Light, including the deep meaning of faith. Understand that:

Faith is causative. Faith dictates.

Faith ordains the universe of your life. If you have no faith, you open the door to the manifestation of Karma since you are moving away from God Principle. To have faith is to take hold of all your power. Since faith is causative, you hold in it the power of Creation. You dictate reality according to the faith you have. For any specific situation if you have 20% faith in it, that thing will manifest for you 20%, if you have 50% faith, it will go as far as 50%. If you have 100% faith, that thing will manifest 100%.

•

When you are agitated panicking about something… first: Stop. Go to your center and say to yourself:

"Faith, God is working"

Remember that famous saying:

"Faith moves mountains"

It is because of all this. Jesus said for this teaching:

"When in doubt… Violet Light, it is pure faith"

•

"Breathe in deeply. Feel the Violet Light surrounding you. Feel how it enters into your body and aura. Feel the power of faith in you. Close your eyes and absorb yourself in the energy of faith."

INVOCATION

Use this invocation any time you feel like you need it. It is very powerful:

"I ask God and the compassion, power, love and wisdom of the Violet Light, that the highest truth is manifested for: ...this situation, person, whatever has to be transmuted... in accordance with the essence of the Violet Light. Thank you." Amen.

You can use it as an aid, as a decree to be said in loud voice. It is not necessary to use it to work with the light, but it is an option you have.

IN SENDING VIOLET LIGHT...

The best will manifest not what your ego wants, because that may not be the best. Hence you must know how to let go; ask and let go. Here the best will always manifest, that is consciousness and the highest vibration – the greatest good for all – not only for you. This is why it is asked that the "best manifests" when invoking Violet Light, and then let go – it is in the hands of God, in the hands of the highest will. And if what you imagined does not happen, accept what is, it is the best for your evolution and that of others.

●

PRACTICES
Healing the past, solving the present

Healing the past

Read all the meditation before starting step by step.

- *Enter into meditation. You can recreate the mystical atmosphere of the other meditations. This will always make the energy stronger.*

- *Invoke the Violet Light to help you heal your past. Do it in the way it comes from your heart.*

- *Concentrate on your breathing.*

- *Let the energy pull you into meditation.*

- *Once you feel connected inside, ask the Violet Light to take you to a situation of your distant past, it can even be from your childhood. A situation in which something has remained unsolved. Something that still affects you.*

- *See that situation like a movie in your mind.*

- *Visualize all the important details: people involved, yourself, the place, words said, feelings, whatever happened.*

- *Put Violet Light in everything and everyone, surrounding the scene with it. See it falling down and enveloping each one there and the events that happened. And don't forget yourself – this is to help heal your trauma and also help heal others'. See the Violet Light entering all the hearts.*

- *Stay there and see what happens.*

- *Allow 10 minutes for it.*

- *Give thanks.*

- *Breathe deeply and slowly three times.*

- *Open your eyes.*

Observe what happened.

What feelings did you have? How do you feel now?
The feelings from the past, have they been transformed?
Did your and others' hearts opened?
Do you feel relieved?

-

I have observed through years of Violet Light courses, that when putting Violet Light into situations of the past, always the Truth comes out. Often the true feelings show up. Conflicts always happen because one of the parts was not coming from truth, and was not sincere with himself: was not showing his true feelings. The Violet Light reveals that hidden truth behind the masks and often in this meditation, the script of the situation changes making the scene become alive. This change of script always manifests a different end, with the associated liberation.

Solving the present

Again, read all the meditation before you start step by step.

- *Enter into meditation.*

- *Invoke the Violet Light to help you solve your present. Do it in the way it comes from your heart.*

- *Concentrate on your breathing.*

- *Let the energy pull you into meditation.*

- *Once you feel connected inside, bring to mind a situation of your present that you are living right now.*

- *Work, relationships, family, something that needs to be solved.*

- *See that situation like a movie in your mind.*

- *Visualize all the details including people, yourself, feelings, the problem, whatever is happening.*

- *Put Violet Light in everything, surround the scene with it. See it falling on the scene.*

- *See the light entering all the hearts.*

- *Stay there and see what happens.*

- *Allow 10 minutes for it.*

- *Give thanks.*

- *Breathe deeply and slowly three times.*

- *Come out of the meditation.*

- *Open your eyes.*

Helping someone

- *Now in meditation, concentrate on a close person that needs help or healing.*

- *Send Violet Light to this person in whatever way comes to you for ten minutes.*

- *Give thanks for being able to help in this way.*

•

A WORD ABOUT CHILDREN

If you have children, what you must take into account is that they are here to realize their Luminous Self. What is important is that they do not become heirs of the limiting belief system, most adults have inherited. Keep them away from lies and unnecessary limitations: do not repress their wave length. Treat them as wise beings, which they are. Listen truly to their message. Do not block their light. Instead seek the means to enhance it and support their high consciousness. They bring great seeds of light. It is fair that you do not make the same mistakes, that were made with you when you were a child. Give them wings, space to fly.

It is excellent to teach children to meditate on the Violet Light. You can meditate together with them before they go to bed, and eventually allow them to do it on their own, sometimes too. When I have done this with children, they flowed beautifully and found it a very magical moment. You can use a simple meditation based on any of the three given, after the main Violet Light Activation. Or you can improvise a simple meditation where they can visualize themselves, surrounded with Violet Light and see this light in their hearts, or above them as a protective, caring presence. They are very open to energies and the Violet Light, as a divine presence, will easily manifest in a natural way for them. This will enhance their light and talents, as well as develop their creativity and keep their hearts open. They will have more concentration in learning, more creativity in playing and also with the arts. They will develop better, as well as enhance their energies through improving their chakras, and the synergy of the two hemispheres of the brain, so they will grow up in a more balanced way.

If they start to meditate soon in life, they will develop their own inner wisdom and will not be easily manipulated by mass unconsciousness, when teenagers or adults. They will also know much better what they want in life, and will be truer to their hearts always. They will be happier children.

PRACTICES FINAL WORD

As a close for this wonderful chapter, I will tell you something that Jesus said to me. The Violet Light comes from the Source of Light of the Universe, from our Divine Father, God. We as human beings are divine, and the divine spark of light is within us. Jesus stressed intensely in the early times of my connection with the Violet Light, to contact the light within, to generate my own light. The idea is that since "I am" a divine spark, "I can" expand my own light so it shines more brightly. Jesus wants that we do not become dependent on the idea of light outside, but that we become co-creators with God by being able to support and work with our own light. In this way we develop our own light and power. His command in this is essentially:

"Generate the Violet Light from within"

So I suggest to you not to forget this, and to give it importance among the other practices you may select from the ones in this chapter. You can see the Light coming from the center of your being, or being generated from your heart. See it becoming more and more intense. Do this every day as you go to work, as you shower or take a walk. You can see the light blazing from your heart or from the heart chakra, or from a deep point in the inner space of your being, whatever feels more natural to you.

It does work. It will happen; you will feel it. Just don't give up at the first tries. Keep doing it and it will gather momentum, clarity and intensity. You will feel its blessings and it will illumine you and your life from within. Remember, at any time connect with the Violet Light from within – radiate it until it is projected beyond yourself.

You can use this invocation:

"Violet Light, allow me to live in your essence. Make of me your permanent dwelling."

Everything is possible

To have all the faith, we have to turn like children. This is why Jesus said that to enter the Kingdom of God, we have to be like them. Children believe anything is possible. It is just that they live in a world of adults that plays tricks on them; a world that does not believe everything is possible. As for their relationship with the rest of the Universe, it is correct. For children, the world of God is very accessible. When you turn like children, you easily access it.

I remember as a child I believed anything was possible – and other kids did too. Then as an adult, I lost some of that. I then worked intensely at generating again in me, the belief in everything. Now with the Violet Light, I have recovered the belief that anything is possible. I have seen it as I have experienced the magic and wonder of God in it. For the light there are no limits, anything can be real, anything can happen. It has surprised me in so many ways. It still does. It is amazing. God is such a creator, playful, a great magician, the Master Alchemist: He can conceive anything and can create anything. All the possibilities are available to Him. That is why when we become again like children, we see as He sees. It is not that children are "innocent," it is that adults do not "see" and therefore believe children are. Children are very close to God and to His limitlessness.

You can therefore work at acquiring the vision of God. The human vision is very limited. Use the help God is giving you. If you have difficulty in believing, or if you just want to see what God is doing, go to the section of experiences at the end of the book, and read how God's love power in the Violet Light made everything possible for so many people.

•

Meditate on the Violet Light long enough, and you will see a magical alchemy manifesting in your life. You will see how your vibration becomes elevated and therefore your consciousness... then anything is possible.

•

"For five minutes, visualize a sun of Violet Light in the center of your forehead."

•

When you are in God connection, you are with God.

You are protected. Do not worry.

You will be guided to be at the right place at the right time.

You do not have to figure it out.

– CHAPTER 14 –

•

A GUIDE TO LIFE'S PATH:
THE PRINCIPLES OF THE VIOLET LIGHT

*"When you look for bliss where
God isn't, He will show you your
deception. Try to understand
His message."*
– Kahan

Although there are many principles to look into and contemplate, in reality there is only one:

"Compassion"

We looked at it in the practices. We now mention it as the overall standpoint from where we should look at life, and the door to that is an open heart.

Compassion is not what it appears at first. We can summarize it as: "the ability to help someone in what he or she truly needs." One way this happens is by putting oneself in the position of the other, and understanding his or her real needs. Someone may ask something of you, but that might not necessarily be what he truly needs. Often the ego in us wants a "sweet" when that is really harming us. The sweet thing is often something in place of reality, a substitute to make life more "agreeable" but more unconscious too. It is something pleasant to avoid facing the truth, and therefore remain deceived for longer. Compassion is not to provide satisfaction to the whims of others, but to provide true service – which is what compassion aims at. More often than not it is the "sour" truth we have to make available to our brother or sister, and we can do it with sweetness too. Every situation is different and what works in one, may not work in another. So discernment has to be used. To exercise compassion therefore, a higher awareness must be activated in us in order to identify the real need behind the mask. Obviously physical needs are more immediate, and when someone is exhausted what he needs is to rest.

Compassion is not about sympathizing with the complacency of someone, but to be firm about what is necessary to move ahead in life. So compassion is not about sympathizing with weakness, it is about promoting strength, life and light, on the way to relieve others from their suffering – their dependency. And this is done from true love. We can say that from this perspective compassion would be: "the true relief of others' suffering," which is a very deep subject – much more than what it appears. In a moment we will see what Buddha's vision is on this.

Sometimes the compassionate way is not acting but just supporting with love and blessings, letting people have their processes. Firm wisdom based on true discernment, is necessary for true compassion to exist. Therefore we are talking about a very fine sword made of light, wisdom and love that needs to be wielded with skill, forged in the inner fire of knowledge of the soul. Of course that is a skill you learn through practice, but specially as your awareness increases and your deception diminishes – something that can be accomplished by being in contact with this energy.

As I mentioned earlier on in the book, Buddha said: "existence is suffering." He did not mean that we are in pain constantly as such. He was referring to the suffering that comes from living in a physical body, which brings with it limitations, ignorance, and not knowing our own true spiritual nature. All that is in itself a great suffering, although not conscious for many most of the time. So compassion being to help reduce the suffering of others, or of oneself, would be directed at increasing their consciousness: the knowledge of their Divine Self. I would put it as: "supporting the freedom of all beings." This would be the highest kind of compassion. The one that aims at the highest good for everyone. That which Buddha aimed at in his teachings.

The Violet Light is therefore about compassion. Just that to free you from suffering, it may "apparently" throw you around sometimes like a big wave would, in order to remove from you the deeply rooted neurotic patterns that cause you so much suffering, and it will do it having no regard for them at all. You might think something in you is being pulled to pieces. It is true. It is called: your ignorance. You are torn away from all that which is not truth or real. So expect lies, illusion, false attitudes, veils, masks, pretension, deception, to be removed from you in the contact with the Violet Light. What the light leaves you with after such uncovering is your truth, your light, your power: love and wisdom.

Compassion means:

- We & Ours
- Greater Cause
- Giving your best to others
- Avoiding harming intentions
- Forgiveness
- Self-observation
- Gentleness
- Being true
- Steadfastness
- Faith
- Being cause
- Dharma
- Transmission
- Peace
- Humility & Gratitude

Let's look at each one of them.

WE & OURS

> *"Today I learn the law of love; that which I give my brother is my gift to me."*
> – A Course in Miracles

This principle is saying that we must change the "I" and "mine," for the "we" and "ours," to break free from the constraint of ego-centered awareness most people live with. Also to open up to the person who is before us, and not exclude him or her from the right to be considered equal to us in all respects, and in so doing to give them the same consideration. Further, we must enter into the consciousness of the brotherhood of all humanity. In leaving behind the small "I" consciousness, you truly begin to see others and their needs, and thus have the revelation of how you can serve them. In serving them, you serve the greater purpose of unity created from a diversity, and you consider others and yourself members of the same family.

GREATER CAUSE

This one is about acting from the highest motive in yourself. Motivation is what creates Karma, so the right motive will generate "good karma." Sometimes a situation may not develop as you had intended and it may end up as nothing, but the motive was right because it was high. The highest motive will generate the highest good. You can then say you are acting from a greater cause. To support the greatest cause is what we should all look for when acting. Greater cause is pitching your motivation at the highest point, that will always be the greatest good for all.

GIVING YOUR BEST TO OTHERS

We have a choice in selecting what we want to give to others from our own selves. It is often too easy to give anything that comes up in response to others, for instance the first reaction that comes to you. But to make sure you always give the best in you, takes more effort and concentration, and especially discipline. We can train our minds to make the best choice, from the attitudes and feelings we have available. No doubt, the best in us will be infused with love and promote consciousness in others. Perhaps you do not feel you can do it, or feel that you cannot do it all the time. Growth requires effort. To become a better human being, you must work at correcting in you the wrong patterns that cause disharmonies. To sow the right seeds takes great care. So I invite all from here to make that effort to generate the necessary discipline. The right seeds will produce a better harvest for the sower and for all.

AVOIDING HARMING INTENTIONS

First, you need to consider avoiding harm to yourself. As you treat yourself, you invariably will treat others. So if you cause harm to yourself, you will not be able to avoid causing harm to others. That is easily seen in self-destructive habits which are often imposed on others, without respecting their right to their freedom of choice. You must also contemplate avoiding causing harm as a result of words or thoughts. Avoid destructive aggression, which includes offensive comments because their only purpose is to cause harm. Finally, you should seek to avoid violence in any form.

To act in those ways you must go inside and reflect on the motivation of your actions, and see those areas in which you do not act from a pure motive: a compassionate one. The reason behind a non-compassionate behavior might be resentment. Your work is to see it, to accept it, and to solve it in the right direction – avoiding the detour of letting your frustration out as an attack on another. What is crucial, is to come from the right intention inside; that is pure motive. Often the end result of things is subject to the many perceptions involved, and we cannot control that. But that should not be an excuse not to come from the right place.

Solving issues positively and advancing in the right direction, is what we want in life. And that means taking responsibility for what is ours, to avoid creating a burden for others with our own unsolved issues. That will only result in creating greater burdens for us. Life is fair; as you solve your issues and lighten your unprocessed burden, you will experience more light, peace and strength. An unknown joy and serenity will be appearing in you.

FORGIVENESS

Forgiveness is a school on its own. We have seen it as a major issue in the teachings of the Violet Light. Here it could not be left out. The first step, is to forgive yourself for any wrong judgment you might have incurred with yourself. Then you are open to forgiving others. The reality is that others are only guilty in our eyes. We have seen that in the eyes of God we are all innocent; we are only lost, confused or unconscious. So the attitude with others is that of forgiving them for not being perfect to our imperfect eyes. In this way we take away our judgments of them and see their innocence. Then you need to forgive life and its circumstances, for whatever wrongdoing you believe it has caused you. The need to forgive is the need of our own peace, because while we keep in an unforgiving attitude, we remain in tension, unhappy and do not experience the freedom of peace.

SELF-OBSERVATION

In order to be aware of these principles you have to observe yourself. Without this quality we are not able to keep ourselves on the right track, and our focus on the alchemical place in our minds which is able to produce the results we need. For that, you need again to ask yourself at any moment: "what is my mind doing?" and in this way be able to see if you are living the principles. In observing yourself, you will catch your mind moving away from them, and you will see when that is happening. Then you will be able to correct your attitude as appropriate. By watching what your mind is doing in any situation, you will know if you are being compassionate, forgiving; if you are giving the best of yourself. As you continue to meditate on the Violet Light, your heart will open more and more and you will naturally fall into the consciousness of the principles.

GENTLENESS

"Gentle is the way of life… gentle is the rhythm of Nature…" The divine energy manifests in Creation through gentleness. It is true that there is also great force in Nature sometimes, but those are specific moments that do not last, but are necessary to keep a balance that often has been altered by man. Gentleness is the general rhythm of things in nature. As Lao Tsu says: "High winds do not last all morning." So it is good to imitate Nature. Gentle ways will always take us to the right place, and will create harmony around us. Let's remember that: "as you sow, so shall you reap," and therefore you cannot expect to bring home serenity, if you have sown tempests. Often mankind misses the point of gentleness and uses force to do things, or to solve problems creating some more problems because the use of force, always creates a reaction. It is like the side effect. The forceful reaction way to approach things many people have, is based on fear. This does not generate harmony. We are all gentle inside as our true nature. Forcefulness is a mask to appear terrible, and therefore a way to protect that true inner vulnerability that has not yet, at large, been fully understood. Gentle strength is a much more effective and powerful force in life. It unites, it solves things without side effects. It heals and brings peace. Its side effects are love and gratitude. This is the wisdom of gentleness, to tune in to the smooth flowing of the Universe. In that way you immerse yourself in the only positive life-enhancing current that will take you to where you need to go. So think how you manage your actions, thoughts and feelings those are the ones that create waves, and see in what areas in you and in your life you can create gentleness. As the philosophy of Tai Chi says: "Gentleness brings harmony, because if you meet force with force, the result will always be conflict; but if one side of the equation brings gentleness to it, it does not matter if the other brings force, the result will always be peaceful."

Gentle ways are based on truth. They run deep. Without that depth of truth, there is no true gentleness. Using the Violet Light will generate a tremendous amount of gentleness – gentle strength – in you as it erases the causes that maintain a forceful and non-creative behavior. Then you will experience a tremendous strength inside... then, what is the need to be forceful?

Reflection point

The other side of this, is that you cannot bring all walls down with sweet words. There are two principles in the Universe that represent the main two polarities: Yin and Yang. Yin is the soft principle and Yang the concentrated power. Yin is lasting; Yang is short and intense. There is a time and place for each. Discernment will be the way to know what that is. I refer in this section to gentleness as a way of being. At specific times, strong will needs to be applied as an action of love. This strength of will comes from love, whereas the forcefulness of the ego comes from fear. Tai Chi practice is slow, gentle, profound. When applied in combat it becomes Kung Fu. In the early times of the art there was a saying: "The Master is the one who knowing the art, never uses it." But when a caravan was attacked by bandits, they always had a Tai Chi Master with them, often "disguised" as a gentle old man who then became a deadly warrior.

So gentleness is the way of living and dealing with everything, unless intensity is required to bring about the desired effects. This intensity will come from spirit not from ego. I have known many great spiritual Masters, well–known for their focused powerful ways in certain circumstances that required it. What this power is looking at is to bring about a greater benefit. Ego power will act out of its own agenda. Spirit power, in service.

Gentleness should be seen as the general way to live, but do not forget the more direct aspect of the Will of God. Sometimes a strong impact is the only way to free a soul or a situation. The Violet Light Grace sometimes is very forceful because, in some instances, this is the only way it will break rigidity down, or open a heart. The vision of gentleness here is about avoiding artificial forcefulness, born out of weakness and not out of love. When forceful energy comes from love, it seeks to bless.

BEING TRUE

The only way you can achieve this is acting from your heart. This has a number of aspects. First, it means that acting from the heart you will be true rather than false, so you will be yourself. Then you have to be real, this is to acknowledge your truth and you talk and act from it. For this you need honesty with yourself; you have to avoid pretension – dropping your masks of pretension to reveal and honor your heart, your truth. To honor your heart therefore, is fundamental. You cannot lie to yourself and not suffer. Honesty is the only way free of charge. Any other way you pay toll. And that means hardship for yourself and others. So honoring the heart is the only sane policy you can follow. In times like these ones in which the planetary vibration is so high, any lies and pretensions you tell yourself, will make you spin so fast giving you such hard time, that you will not want to keep lying to yourself.

The Violet Light reveals to you the truth inside you, and consumes anything that is covering it trying to pretend you are something you are not, thus revealing your true feelings. Being yourself, you will meet heart with heart. This is true communication and the result of it is unity.

STEADFASTNESS

A tree bends in the wind to concede its initial position, but it has a fixed point in the roots that anchors it to the ground. You also must have a fixed point in yourself, so you can flow like the tree in the wind being able to adapt, but with that anchor that stops you from loosing your center. That point is your inner wisdom. From it comes discernment, that quality that will tell you how much you can bend without losing yourself. You need this quality because if you want to advance in your life, you need steadfast work but also conviction in your work. You need steadfastness to adhere to the principles; you need it to live a harmonious life. You will progress according to the degree of steadfastness you exercise. And at the end of the day, it is only that commitment to doing right that will bring results – led by Grace of course. Any other way of walking will produce no effects, it will be useless.

A steadfast attitude is the perfect balance for the fickle and whimsical nature of the mind, which is a sure way of getting nowhere and achieving nothing worthwhile. Steadfastness is the way to give root and steadiness to a very chaotic and undisciplined energy that rules our lives. Steadfastness is developed in contact with the Violet Light, since its influence stabilizes the mind and produces a deep inner wisdom, which is in itself a real root in anybody's life.

FAITH

We have talked about faith but being such an important subject, I must include it with the principles. This serves two purposes: one is to look at it again from our developed awareness at this point of our journey, and the other is to remind ourselves of its importance. Now the emphasis is on the vision of it as the solid ground which supports your life. It is therefore closely related to steadfastness. It provides steadfastness with the solid and fertile ground on which to develop. It is the bedrock upon which steadfastness grows. I have seen in my therapies and in life, people developing insights through their inner work and doubting themselves afterwards, because of lack of faith in themselves and in the revelations granted. That lack of faith did not allow at the time to solidify the wisdom in them, and therefore they could not generate the steadfastness that was coming along. When something valid is not rooted in our consciousness, growth is impossible. Others take the issue to extremes making doubt a way of living. This lack of faith creates such a hole in their consciousness, that all inner work is useless. The positive effects of the work are not rooted in their consciousness. Those effects are meant to be the building blocks of your own inner temple: the steps on the way to your own elevation and freedom. Believe is what we are made of. If we do not believe we are made of nothing, because nothing will stick to us. As Jesus said: "Such will be their lives, as they believe."

BEING CAUSE

As human beings we need to move to the consciousness of being cause. Often the view of a person of himself is that of a victim of causes outside him. This is not the truth. We are cause, not effect. We are creators of what happens to us. Then there will be some who will say: "I didn't do anything for such event to happen to me..." That is just apparently true, but it is not the truth. The truth of the matter is that someone did something for that event to happen to him or to her;

it is just a matter of recognizing what was done that caused the event – or what was thought or felt, since they are the creative forces. At the end, it all comes down to vibration. You attract things, people and events to you according to your general vibration. That includes the way you might be vibrating at any specific time. We saw that principle earlier in the book. So even if you are at home doing nothing actively, you will attract like a magnet whatever it is that the vibration of your thoughts is putting out. So you are cause.

We know by now vibration is the first principle of Creation, the first creative principle. It is from it that things manifest themselves. It is the magic of God in each of us. You want to work magic? you just need to vibrate in a particular manner and that will manifest. Of course the clearer you are in your mind, the more evolved you are and the more united to the Universal Source – the more control of that magic you will have. What may impede your dreams to manifest is the amount of interference in you – negative thoughts – because they will be manifesting until they are cleared, because they also vibrate in a frequency. The Violet Light will clear those negative thought patterns, and leave your mind clear to think and vibrate in the highest frequencies of love, joy and self-esteem. These will be the seeds that will produce the best harvests for you. So you are the creator of what happens to you. You only have to develop the consciousness that you are cause, and understand why you attract what you do to your life. You have to assume that what you sow, you will reap.

DHARMA

This Sanskrit word has a lot of meaning for us. It refers to "right action" – that which does not create Karma. So it is an action that is enlightened because it contemplates the highest principles in the Universe: it is taking the best choice at any moment. So we can say, that to look for peace, harmony and love in action, is to live in Dharma. When your acting brings the situation the closest to the

Divine, we can talk of Dharma. "How would God act?" would be a good question for that.

If you do not live in Dharma, you create Karma. So the way to Dharma would be generating harmony, peace, conditions of life proper for life's development that also benefit the life of others. It is about treating the fluid of energy of the Universe, with care and respect. Instead of creating agitation, it is about becoming a channel for the Highest Will. Something equivalent to "getting out of the way." Then you can create harmony. Since there is no will greater than God's, if you are not aligned with His, you won't have the best outcome possible for you, so you would be "on the way." God really supports the highest will for yourself, but if you haven't realized that when yours does not pursue the best for you, God let's you have it your way since He respects your free will. When that causes you trouble, you can choose again and then move on to better choices until you choose the best for you. Then you are thinking as God thinks. Then you are in Dharma. You will therefore be far better off than ever for finally you have accepted God's will for you: all the treasures God has in store for you. Again the Violet Light being infused completely with the Will of God, will help you situate your life in line with that greater will. It will transmute the small vision of yourself liberating you from your need of and addiction to it, setting you free. Taking you to Dharma.

God promotes that we accept to be in the "I Am" presence all the time – the only place of total joy and freedom. If we can accept that, we will have it. In the same way, if we can accept our healing we will have it. That is God's will for us. Of course that might take some time while everything that is not aligned with it, turns that way. But the sooner you start, the sooner it will happen. God does not punish you – He does not want you to suffer. If you can see that and accept it, you will move into a new dimension of living: you will be free from limitations and will find peace. It is our own neurotic, distorted thinking that keeps those limiting suffering conditions operating, and the belief that God might have wanted that for us. Nothing further from the truth. God is our best ally and friend. It is time we realize that. It is time to start living in Dharma.

TRANSMISSION

Light is for all. If you have it, you will share it. It is inevitable. If it is in you, it will radiate from you. The level of light active in you, will impregnate your actions, your words. Share your light with others so you help them open their hearts more, and you move them towards finding greater peace in themselves. Let them know the presence of Grace, as you discover that Grace and its effects on you. Transmit and expand the Grace of the Violet Light.

PEACE

> *"Your free will is your ability*
> *to choose ultimate peace."*

"Live in the peace that is inside you." Peace is already within. No amount of searching for it outside will make it any closer to you than what it is now. To experience what is already there, all that is not peace must be removed. The Violet Light does this beautifully. In the meantime, or while that is happening in you, you should aim at creating peace within and without by all means available. To do this you can focus on the idea that you must always choose the path that takes you to peace, as much as possible – taking the choices that bring peace. From this viewpoint life becomes very simple and the choices of life too: you choose peace. Away from any other considerations of life, the choices you make are not any more in terms of acquiring something, but in terms of: "Will this choice bring the greatest peace to me and others?"

From this place you will never go wrong. The first immediate result of this might not be peace but a process that might bring some shifts, sometimes uncomfortable, in order that true peace can be met at the end of it. Don't lose the perspective that the right choice for greater peace, will often bring a shaking process that doesn't precisely look like peace, but it is necessary to get to it. Make peace choices with discernment.

●

We have seen that the Violet Light brings the consciousness of these principles. This means that they are in it. Therefore as you meditate more and more on the Violet Light, the principles will be manifesting in you as part of your Self. The point is to do that and also to work intently in your daily life, to make the principles conscious for you. As you do so you will be a better ground for the Violet Light to anchor itself more fully and profoundly into your Self. So you see that one way helps the other. The following are two areas of great importance in the vision of the Violet Light, that deserve a separate treatment.

●

"Visualize at any time a sphere of
Golden Light within your heart,
inside a violet flame."

HUMILITY & GRATITUDE

Humility

Humility is one of the most important qualities in life. Without it you are closed and if you are closed, the goodness and Grace of God and of the Universe, cannot enter you. One of the ways in which those arrive at you, is through your brothers and sisters in your daily life. Lack of humility is the worst thing you can have. From it ego is born, and the obnoxious attitude that God is not necessary – and hence the false and distorted believe that you have all power without the Creator. In this way pride and the sense of self-importance grow, on the way to self-destruction. Humility is the acknowledgement that it is Him who sustains everything – it is Him who sustains you. He is your creator, your power and strength come from Him.

What place is there for pride, for self-importance? Merit and the applause are for Him. This is not an attitude of "I am nothing," "I have no value." This is low self-esteem. It is not about that. It is an attitude of "I am worth all," "I am all" in union with Him – thanks to Him, and recognizing Him always. This is your protection before pride and ego: "I am not the doer, He is through me: my merit lies in how much I allow Him to manifest through me." He is noble and pure – created everything out of love – and in His infinite humility, He didn't even sign it. You won't find a leaf on a tree in the forest … you turn it around to see it says: *"God. Created in 1847" or "Creation, by God."* Let's use this example as the definition of humility: "Total absence of self-importance."

Gratitude

The Universe moves through gratitude. It is another door that allows things to manifest in your life. From humility gratitude is born, which is the acknowledgement that you have been and are blessed with the divine gifts: infinite abundance, the perfection, the love, the beauty, and the power of God. You receive it all, you recognize it in humility and offer your gratitude – you give thanks.

Pride and self-importance do not let people recognize where all that comes come from, and how fortunate they are. In offering your gratitude, you honor the act of receiving, you honor the gift and he who gives. Then, since you appreciate it you receive more. That is the opening of the door: you have made space for blessings to enter. If there is no gratitude there is no acknowledgment of God and of His gifts, and since you don't appreciate nor value what you have – what you have been given – you are not given more. What for, if you are not going to appreciate it? Not only that, you also lose what you have. This is not a punishment from God, it is a practical law of the Universe. If you have a cup full and you don't drink from it, the cup remains full and no more abundance can enter into it. This is the: "you are not given more." Still water is spoiled – it rots. This is the: "you lose what has been given to you." And in the pride of ingratitude as: "I have all power, I don't need anything," people don't drink from the source and dry up – so they die. This is a consciousness death.

An open and well-nourished heart in gratitude, is always plentiful and joyful. From plenitude comes giving. So we see that from gratitude, comes service. Because giving from plenitude is serving. Hence, God in His plenitude serves all, all the time. We must be like Him, because we are one with Him. So in serving, we come closer to Him. In gratitude we preserve the things of life and we take care of what we have: body, home, abundance, relationships, wisdom, love, light... we preserve life, this is mercy, and in doing that we do something useful, practical: an offering to God for what we are. We said this was a very practical issue: the Universe does not throw energy away, it gives use to everything. One of the ways in which the Universe gives is through opportunities – opportunities to grow, to evolve, to heal, to become free – all that which you yearn for. It is the acknowledgement of those opportunities what makes you take them. It is gratitude.

●

*"Feel gratitude for everything
God has given you, for all that
you are and have. Bless all
that with Violet Light."*

– CHAPTER 15 –

•

SEEING BEYOND OURSELVES

> *"There is nothing more important*
> *and greater in life than to be*
> *a channel for God's Grace."*
> – Kahan

THE RIGHT ATTITUDE

At the moment of applying the practices act with detachment. This is exercising the excellent practice of karma yoga: detachment from results.

Karma = Inertia

Karma can be seen in this way. Thus Karma needs to be transmuted to create consciousness, since inertia is unconscious behavior. Such behavior creates Karma. So the circle is perpetuated. Transmutation allows you to break free from the circle, to start acting anew and from conscious choice illuminated in your own discerning light.

Karma yoga can be seen as right action free from results. Free because you don't consider them. They are left to God. You do the right thing and the results are in Him, the fruits of the action are His. This is the way to act. Otherwise your acting is tainted with selfishness. And even in service you are looking for your reward. This is obviously not service. It does not mean the rewards won't come, and the abundance won't be generated, of course they will, but we do not act because of them, we act because it is the best for all, because sending Violet Light to someone will truly improve his life and accelerate his evolution, expanding his consciousness: we want to help. We act in service because what we know or have can help others and, we share that love and knowledge. But we are a "channel" for it and that is the way it works; that is why it works: His are the merits and the recognition, since:

"His is the Kingdom, the Power and the Glory"

Remember that always, and you will be saved from the deceitful domains of the ego. Acting while forgetting this will only inflate your ego in the worst way: that which claims self-importance on the grounds of "spiritual service."

When you are serving with the Light, the power is borrowed from God and the applause is for Him, because His is the Kingdom – He created it. Believe me, you do not want to feed your ego because that will be your greatest obstacle in your progress: while you are thinking you are "very enlightened," you will miss the reason why you are going around in circles. You won't attain any degrees that way. You might not be conscious of that manipulation, but the Universal Consciousness is: the doors to The Kingdom are only opened in the presence of true love and humility. So when acting with the Violet Light act without selfishness; you do not act for your own self-interest when helping others. Make a point and an effort to understand that. To do it fully might take you work and years, but the effort is worthwhile, one of the best investments you can make. In this way we become a channel for God's Grace and for Universal Compassion. There is nothing more important in life.

PERSEVERANCE

Perseverance is invincible. It conquers everything. There are unbalances that require more time to be healed. If you use the Violet Light for something and you see that it does not become balanced, you have to keep on, it is a deeply rooted issue and probably it has been like that for a long time. Its resolution is being accelerated with the Violet Light, but it needs greater dosage. Keep your faith and your good work alive.

•

At any moment...

At any moment you can ask yourself what you can do to advance in your daily life:

- Repeat the mantra "I Am" or "I Am the Resurrection and the Life."

- Repeat your own personal mantra if you have one.

- Connect yourself with the Violet Light.

- Meditate on it.

- Remember God.

- Remember your spiritual guides and Masters.

- Ask their loving guidance and help.

- Desire your illumination and that of others.

- See with the eyes of love.

- See how you can help others.

FIVE KEYS FOR THE CHANGE OF CONSCIOUSNESS

These points are essential for your change: the steps and the places to be in a changing era.

We and our world
You already know them. We need to move from the contracted awareness of the "I." Living life from the "we" consciousness, we work together for the same goal, beyond individual agendas: the ascension of humanity as a group.

Impeccability
Live by this standard and you will have nothing to worry about. It is about being transparent with your motivations, before yourself and God.

We are One = Love
Live being aware of this. It is where we have to go: destination.

Experience of the Absolute
Life is about uniting your consciousness with the Absolute Divine Consciousness of the Universe — Brahman — and knowing you and It are one. Seek this experience as you meditate and in your daily life. This is the greatest; this is all. We must seek this; nothing else will fulfill us or give us true peace. This is what has transcendence beyond ordinary life.

Acting in service
"The greatest good for the greatest number." This came out before. Take it as a key to greater consciousness you must never forget. It is the banner of every person or nation who really wants to be part of the new times, because this way of being creates the new consciousness every day of our lives.

•

"See your heart united with everybody's heart,
through beams of Violet Light. Send Violet
Light to close ones, to humanity and the planet."

TRANSPERSONAL CONSCIOUSNESS

In transcending the "I" and "mine," you come upon a transpersonal reality. This is the essential message of Aquarius in the age of its name: the breaking away from individuality to touch Universality. And then the merging into that Universality – the Source of all wisdom, love and unity. It is clear, to do that we must live and go through profound changes individually and collectively. It will happen, the energies and frequencies from above are already set to that end. It is already happening. Here the message of the French Revolution comes alive like never before: "Liberte" "Egalite" "Fraternite" – Freedom, Equality, Brotherhood. We must prepare ourselves to enter this new consciousness and truly live a life of transpersonal consciousness.

A transpersonal Universe is what we live in. One in which all you do and all you think affects others, affects the planet, affects the Universe. We must become aware of this because we are responsible for the effects of all we do – feel, think, say and act – of all we are creating. We are all united and whatever we do affects others. We must learn to act with the greatest consciousness and responsibility.

We cannot shut ourselves away and think negative thoughts, pretending that because we are alone we can do what we please because we won't affect anybody. This is not true. And it has never been so. But it is time we all become aware of it. As Saint Germain has said many times, we are responsible for the wrong use of all the energy that has gone through us. If we think negatively in solitude, we indeed are sending that vibration to the world. If we think thoughts of love, we are affecting the field of energy of everyone too. So we can't escape influencing the Universe from our own home.

Understanding this you can understand how you meditating and being in contact with the energy of the Violet Light, can positively affect the whole world. It is crucial that the greatest amount of people enter into contact with this high frequency of light, at this planetary moment. This is the message of the Masters responsible for this sector of the Universe. The blessings this energy brings are infinite: God knows what He is doing. The intention here is not to acquire followers but to create free beings. The deep desire from the Masters and myself in teaching this, is not worship or affiliation of any kind, it is that you and all become like us: free.

THE PURPOSE OF LIFE

> *"Life is not about being nice.*
> *It is about being true. Then*
> *you can be kind."*

"Everything is love"

God is love. The only law in the Universe is love. That's why Saint Agustin said: "Love and do what you want" What is important in life? truly important? Love. But how much do you think about becoming a better lover? Not in a partnership, as a human being, as someone who loves. The measure of your life is love, for as a friend of mine said: "If every day you love more, you are doing fine."

The Ascended Masters have said:

"The only real thing is love. Everything else is not real."

Before such powerful statements, we can only accept we know little of the Truth and we know not much about love, therefore we do not know a lot about God. We can see here – and I advise you not to close your eyes before something so amazing – the fact that we really think life is about anything else but love. We live lives that take us to fame, wealth, having fun, accumulating possessions, self-importance, as if all that was really important. But how many of us often think that life is about love? We are not taught that. We are often taught the opposite and when we are adults, who is teaching that? If most human beings grew the same way, how can we learn? Then the need for Enlightened Masters, Tibetan Lamas, Hindu Gurus, Ascended Masters, or other Illumined individuals that have seen and followed a parallel life and found the reality behind all life.

What if you never thought that, and now you found me telling you this? What if the purpose of all life was to know and understand love and to give it? How wrong would that make the world seem… well, it is. But while everyone at large is pursuing some outside object, big corporations make riches out of it, including states and the world powers, in a race of fulfillment that never fulfills anyone and leaves you empty in more than one sense, lonely and lost… and then what?…

LIFE IS OVER…

Then you will see things that you did not see here and that not many told you about. Then you will remember these words about love. You will understand many things that nobody here wants you to, or simply they might, like you, not know. Then you will thank people for opening your eyes and telling you these things, while you were still alive. Then… you will meet beings of light (yes they do exist) on other planes of existence, and you will be asked in some way or another how you are getting on with the issue of love, in terms of the life you have just finished. So, in one word, the hierarchies that rule the Universe and that are responsible for helping people in their evolution, value above anything else the health of the heart, and that is measured by the degree of openness of it: the amount of love alive in it. Then it is late to realize that life is about love. The time to do it is now, so that you use the most important part of your energy and time, to master what is most important to God. He is the Creator, He knows what transcends death. He is Love. Since you in essence are one with Him, your essence is also love, and if you have not exerted yourself to get to discover what you are about, then you are not in good business, because that means you have spent your lifetime doing whatever it was, but which has kept you in ignorance as to the true purpose of your life, and therefore served as a distraction to it. Because the true purpose of your life is getting to know yourself, your true Self, away from personalities, acquired identities, roles and concepts.

So if you work... fine. If you are married, love your partner. If you play music, feel delirious about it... but whatever it is you do in the engagements of the world, work every day within you to open your heart to unconditional love, because that is the name of the game. This issue about love is far deeper than what appears to be, far more than being "loving." It is about true love, and that is a real path to mastery of life and of yourself. We are all in it. The whole Universe is a University of love. It is our work to advance in it and to reach the depths of understanding of what this universal loving essence means. It is a real enterprise of real work. Put Violet Light in your heart every minute of the day if necessary, because your heart might be closed, or partially so. But do not miss this opportunity to get into action in the right direction.

•

"See your heart surrounded by
soft Violet Light. Feel its sweetness."

"I felt love, peace, tenderness, compassion, power.
The Light brought all these to me."
— Participant of the course.

THE MESSAGE FROM MOTHER EARTH

We are in a global time of Ascension. This means a rising in vibration, an elevation of our personal and global frequency and consciousness. This is happening all around the planet, not just to one or some individuals. The Earth itself has entered into a profound process of rising vibration. This can be felt in many natural places: the Earth is in a state of grace.

Between my working hours writing or giving courses, I have daily taken time to go into some of those natural places, and find a spot in which I can touch the Earth. Sometimes I sit on a rock on top of the cliffs, walk along a deserted beach, or meditate on a natural volcanic rise and feel the high vibration of the Earth. This always feels wonderful. There is a presence of strong energy. I can feel love, peace and power. Often I can perceive a lot of light. The vibration feels stronger than in those places cut off from sky and earth, by "civilized" structures. This is all you need to experience it, to find a natural spot and with your feet on the earth and with an open sky over your head, you will experience the vibration of the Earth.

This tells us that the Earth is vibrating at a very high rate. This means Mother Earth is increasing its consciousness, since the Earth is a conscious being also expanding its awareness. This is something that we are not aware of in general, in the middle of cities or if the only places we visit are the office and home. So this is a message to all to seek direct contact with Mother Earth in a new way. To many, daily life does not offer that possibility, unless it is specifically looked for. We must do it. We must go out of our way to do it. It is very important since in doing it we become healed, balanced, rejuvenated, we enter into peace and recover the natural rhythms of the Earth in us, which we have lost by living such artificial lives away from Nature. In this way, we will experience a connection with the planet that will offer us more tolerance, humility and meaning of life, because it all comes naturally with being in touch with the Earth. Hidden wisdoms and abilities, new inner visions become opened for us in that contact that reveals something magical and mystical, we were cast away from a long time ago.

The Earth has a message to all. Its vibration is raising and it is definitely going up to the realms of spirit, of high consciousness, light and unity: a dimension of harmony and peace that it has not known for millennia. It deserves it, and we do too.

Her call and message is simple:

"Join me in this ascension to the higher planes where we can all live in harmony, peace and love as one consciousness. Casting away negativity, destruction and hate – in a word, separation. Come join me in the final journey to unity."

•

LIGHT PETITION

"I ask for Light for all,
I ask for the Ascension of all.
I forgive, let go and love,
And I carry the Golden Light within the heart."
— Amen

This prayer came down in Mexico, in a meditation with the Earth in a sacred natural place.

It is a prayer for these times. It points the way to go.
It was handed down by the Spirit of Mother Earth, in resonance with Cosmic Mother Consciousness represented by Mother Mary. It should be lived by and decreed any time in meditations and prayers, alone or together, at home or in holy places.

In doing it, its powerful vibration will impregnate the place and the energy field of the Earth, like a call which will resonate more and more in people's hearts. It can be said three times at once or more. It can also be said using "we" instead of "I".

The Golden Light refers to the inner Divine Light in everyone, the Luminous Self in the heart.

•

– CHAPTER 16 –

•

OUR BEST FRIENDS:
THE ASCENDED MASTERS

> *" The only difference between a*
> *Master and a disciple, is that the*
> *Master has surrendered to God."*
> – Kahan

When talking about high spiritual energies, we inevitably have to talk about the high Masters of Light that always accompany them: The Ascended Masters.

These Masters have become so by their degree of fusion with the Divine Light, realizing their total unity with God. They channel complete Divine Consciousness, are free from Karma and have liberated themselves from the constraints and clutch of the ego. Therefore they manifest Christ Powers and Christ Love: the qualities of the Luminous Self. There are many examples of them. Jesus might be one of the closest. Another is Saint Germain, Kotoomy, who in one of his incarnations was Saint Francis. Others are: El Morya, Kwan Yin, Lady Nada and of course the Virgin Mary.

Moving completely away from any relation with the Church, these beings of light act independently of any religious doctrine. Their doctrine is love. They do not know about religious differences. They might manifest somehow through the Christian or other religions that invoke them, but we have to realize at this stage that the Church did not create them and that they are independent of it. You can access them directly in your own personal way without having to conform to any specific religion, and they will respond to you directly and independently of your spiritual beliefs, or even if you do not relate to any spiritual structure. It is the reality, as I also contact Buddha and other deities from Buddhism and I am not Buddhist. Holy personalities are universal. Divine Grace does not belong to a specific spiritual or religious path; Divine Grace is universal. Although every true spiritual path has a different flavor of that Divine Grace. The access to holy personalities and their Grace depends on the openness of heart and on the purity of the individual. It is a mistake often made to consider holy beings exclusive of a specific spiritual path. Whereas the holy figure emanates his or her holy radiance of Grace and blessings to anybody regardless of religious backgrounds, wherever it might be. One of the most beautiful sights I have shared in holy places, has been that of Hindu people visiting Virgin Mary in her sanctuary in Lourdes, France.

Fully enlightened Masters and Saints from any spiritual path, essentially attain the same state of unity with the Divine. So we could include Buddha as well in this section of Ascended Masters, and any other names which manifest this divine state. The key here is that every human being has the God seed within him or her, and this seed can be awakened and taken to full realization. It is the Presence "I Am" the Higher Self of everyone, and it is independent of sex, culture, age, religion or any other aspect of the outer personality. So any human being can develop his consciousness to become an ascended master, and we all should because this is what we are human for.

Ascended Masters work with different frequencies of the Divine Light and help other beings that are not merged into God Consciousness, attain that state: ourselves. This is important because that is our real state. We are living a farce, believing we are something else. This is why they are our best friends. No one in the Universe or upon the Earth, is more interested in and dedicated to our own evolution and well-being than them. Their help is timely and miraculous, their support knows no limits and their love and power are offered always in serving the highest good for everyone. They are always waiting to be called upon. We need to talk about three of them here.

JESUS – THE SPIRITUAL REBEL

We know Jesus well in occidental culture. We often hear him in the Bible. He is in the churches of the Christian and Catholic religions… but he is much more than that. The Church is not the only place to find him, and established religion is not the only way to access him.

I call him "Spiritual Rebel" because it is from spirit that he showed the falseness of the world in which people lived, and his rebellion against all that, which they held so dearly, was the message of freedom he brought with him.

Jesus came to dismantle the system and the slavery of the individual due to ignorance and lies, to bring inner freedom: the system is supported by the deceit within the individual. He rebelled against the system and against every symbol and person who supported it. He did not please them, as he did not agree with their ways. He did not support their world of deceit and pretension at all, and presented such a threat to it with his divine power and love, that shook everyone completely. He clearly showed the lies in which their power was based, as they pretended to be supporting the truth: they were only concerned with their own little accommodated truth, to serve their own purposes and agendas. Before truth all else falls. This is why the establishment was so scared of him. It was so terrified that they crucified him, thinking that this was his end. It was their end, He soared high showing the powers of God in him in his resurrection.

And he is back. His teachings and presence are alive now, more than ever. His consciousness and his energy are here to bring the resurrection of the Christ in all of us. It is he who is behind all the world's upheaval. He has come to shake it again in its final awakening. The spiritual rebel has come to finish the work He started 2000 years ago. In cosmic time, this is a wink. The Violet Light he brings through this and other sources, is one of the main energies of Spiritual Grace that the Great Spirit offers the Earth and the Universe, at this time for global resurrection. Jesus walked the Earth two thousand years ago, but he is still involved with people and life on this planet. Since those times physically here, he has been teaching and evolving in his own right.

My connection with Jesus is direct. It has nothing to do with the church establishment and does not come from this life. Therefore my communication with him is independent of any religious system. When I was a child, his presence was very strong with me always. I remember seeing his face in my mind very clearly, he was very present. My relationship with him was like that of two close friends. When I lived in Mexico, I stayed for a while in a big house full of arches and colonial atmosphere. At night I used to walk the many halls of the house. I lit candles and meditated. I had a relationship with the house and the spaces; the place was alive. One night I started to feel a strong luminous presence near me. I immediately recognized him. It was Jesus. He stayed there and I could feel his presence and vibration; it was very strong. He appeared in that way for a number of nights. We communicated in silence through energy. I found it natural for him to be there. Although I was well away from my childhood years, it was the first time I felt him in that way. He was almost physical. Since then I have experienced his presence with me in a new way. He is constantly present and manifests in many different ways. He is always present in the courses of the Violet Light, and many have reported seeing him in them, or having spiritual experiences with him. Even after the courses many have developed a new strong bond with him.

His life is one of the greatest examples of transmutation, something he manifested constantly and that had its peak moments in his own transfiguration and resurrection.

SAINT GERMAIN –
THE MASTER OF FREEDOM

Traditionally, he has been known as the Ascended Master responsible for the Cosmic Ray of Violet Light. Every ray of Divine Light has a group of beings representing the work and the spiritual energy of that light. Within that group, the highest figure is the Ascended Master. Saint Germain is the head figure of the Violet Ray. He became so by his own merits in working towards the freedom of souls. So to talk of the Violet Light means inevitably to talk of this highly evolved being.

Well known in metaphysical work and literature, this gentle noble and powerful soul, has had a profound spiritual trajectory in the search of spiritual freedom for himself and others. His work and knowledge of the Violet Light is widely seen through his mention of the Violet Flame in many of his books. His: "Golden Book" and "The Seventh Ray" among others, contain mentions of the Violet Flame. The second one is in fact, an overall vision of the mission of the Violet Light for this era upon the Earth. I was surprised when I came upon it, since it speaks of my work and that of others with the Violet Light in these times. I remember a Violet Light course in the north of Spain. In the activation meditation Saint Germain was present in the center of the circle. The atmosphere was deep and profoundly sacred. The spiritual energy was so potent it was indescribable. He in deep silence radiated intense Violet Light to all there. We were deeply transformed by this. I realized he is very close to the Great Divine Spirit and that he has been deeply blessed by Him.

Although he is the Ascended Master officially responsible for the Violet Light, that does not exclude other Ascended Masters from intervening in the work of the Violet Light. Jesus and Saint Germain are working together as a team to bring the Violet Light with its new frequencies to the Earth. They often work together across space and time. Other Masters are working with them to support this huge spiritual event for the planet. Archangels are also part of this work. Including the well-known Archangel Michael, who is taking a predominant role in supporting this work in many ways. Note that Archangel Michael's essential ray of light is the Blue Ray, the ray of the Will of God. This shows that regardless of their main spiritual vibration, any being of light can support another spiritual vibration if the spiritual event manifesting through it, is of cosmic importance, as it is the case with the present emanation of the Great Spirit for Mother Earth.

VIRGIN OF GUADALUPE – THE LADY OF MERCY

Insisting on the point of names and origins, the fact that we use apparent Christian related terminology does not condition these loving beings of light. They are not bound by any religion. They are not Christian, Hindu or anything. They are just beings of light, here to help us. We use their names as they appeared on Earth at one time, and that helps us to identify and relate to them. To my understanding, Mother Mary's essence is the same Universal Mother as Kuan Yin, of the Chinese tradition and Avalokiteshwara the deity of compassion of the Tibetan Buddhism, or other Mother related spiritual beings.

Virgin Mary is a high being of light. All the Virgin appearances are really the same Virgin Mary, but at the time and because of the conditions of the place, she manifested in different ways even through different names. In this case we have Virgin Mary of Guadalupe, as she called herself when she appeared in Mexico City five hundred years ago. The gospels of the apparition mention that when she appeared to a humble man called Juan Diego, she asked for a temple to be built in that place from which she could give mercy. The temple, at first refused by the Christian authorities of the time, was finally built. This change of mind happened when she superimposed her image on Juan Diego's cape, before the incredulous eyes of the Church's hierarchy. That is the miracle of Virgin of Guadalupe. Whether that was the case or not, the truth is that the temple, or rather the "Basilica," that bears her name in Mexico City does give out the energy of mercy: Violet Light. It has been felt and seen by many.

When I was in the Basilica of Guadalupe I felt Virgin Mary's spiritual presence. This was before I knew anything about the Violet Light. The power of love and light that emanates from her there is impressive. The place transforms anyone visiting it, and that is why millions of pilgrims go there every year. In my own experience there, I consider it one of the most powerful places on Earth. I was totally filled with light when I was in it; the vibration is so strong that made me feel a comfortable "dizziness," as I was filled with the Grace that falls on that holy place. I have had reports from people that have seen violet light coming down on the Basilica, some knew about the light there, some didn't. Many people, myself too, have seen or felt the Virgin's presence in the activation courses of the Violet Light. Her love is so strong that, you melt in it. You feel blessed with divine love and light. For us she represents the spiritual figure, that presides over the Violet Ray of Light in its main Earth anchoring: the Basilica of Guadalupe. She also represents the embodiment of Divine Mercy.

Spiritual places we all know about

Santiago de Compostela is another pilgrimage place very famous, situated in the North West of Spain. Pilgrims walk the well-known "Camino de Santiago" the way of Saint James. Lourdes in France is also a world famous place. People go there to receive the energy of healing and many miraculous healings have taken place there.

What is happening in those places? We are not talking about anything new but of something that has always been there and we have known about... but never knew why. Those places are anchors of spiritual energies that radiate their benevolent force blessing the Earth and humanity. Lourdes hosts the "Green Ray of Light" which is the energy of healing, so people there become healed. It makes all the sense. If the energy there was the "Ray of Mambo," people would dance overcome by a greater dancing force... but it is not, it is the energy of healing so it has healing effects.

Spiritual rays of light are anchored onto world famous places like Taj Mahal in India or Lasha, Tibet. This is why those places attract so many people. It is not just the architectural beauty of the places, it is the presence they emanate. I had the opportunity to visit Taj Mahal not long ago. I was impressed by its energy. Something many may not know is that the structure is empty. It is not a palace or a temple, it is a sacred structure that houses three tombs. Inside it is all empty space – apart from those three small tombs. I stayed there on the grounds and gardens for hours, embracing the beautiful loving energy radiating from the place. I watched people. I wondered why after taking their pictures they stayed there for hours around an empty building. Then it dawned on me: it was for the same reason I stayed, they felt so good there. People were so happy, they were having a great time. It is the energy there; it is contagious. I have heard from good metaphysical sources that Taj Mahal is the main Earth anchoring of the energy of spiritual love: the Pink Ray of Light. I have no doubt of this after being there. I could feel it.

The relevance of those places is known to all. We are talking here about some of the most important pilgrimage places in the world. Something truly goes on there. People don't go to Santiago de Compostela by the millions every year, because someone centuries ago decided it was a good idea and created an empty tradition out of it. People are sensitive; they know. What has kept people going for centuries to Lourdes, the Basilica of Guadalupe, Santiago, Taj Mahal, Tibet, and other places is that there is an spiritual reality there, they can touch and feel. Inside the pilgrim or the casual visitor something is touched, a chord struck. The human soul is moved to another dimension, raised to contact a higher spiritual frequency that perhaps cannot be explained, but it can be felt and it is transforming. A human being is put in touch with the transcendental: the divine reality that pulsates inside him. At that moment he is taken out of the ordinary existence to have a glimpse or perhaps much more, of the eternity and the ecstasy of his soul. So it is not surprising people visit them constantly as they look for a healing experience, or a greater spiritual connection.

Going back to the Virgin of Guadalupe, in one of the messages from the Ascended Masters that periodically come from this source, Virgin of Guadalupe invited all: "To carry a heart of Amethyst," a heart of mercy, since the Amethyst is the stone of the Violet Light. It is a violet-colored quartz crystal. In this message she tells all to have mercy in their hearts.

In one of the Violet Light courses in Mexico, a wonderful lady who works with Virgin Mary received this message from her at the end of the course:

"This is the moment to be in the light of infinite love of Mother Earth and the Universe. With all my infinite love to each one of you, I have you close, very close to me. Embrace the Light of the Divine Energy, the entering of the light of the Holy Spirit, Christic Violet Light, the flame of purity and Transmutation. These are times to unite mind and heart, the Triple Flame."

Your Mother from heaven,
Mary

The triple flame is part of the light of the Christ. It is in the heart.

●

I invite you to feel the presence of these three Ascended Masters. Invoke them, talk to them, these or any other Saint you feel close to. Feel what they bring you; ask for their help. They are your best friends and they are very close now. They are helping us with Grace and higher teachings for our evolution. If we open up, we can receive them. Leave doubts, judgments aside; it is time we recover our connection with the extraordinary reality, with the spiritual realm and their beings. We belong there. Connect with them and they will manifest for you.

●

"Enter for a moment into your inner serenity.
Feel the emanation of Grace the Ascended
Masters pour down on you. See it a soft
Violet Light enveloping you completely.
Feel gratitude for their love and support."

– CHAPTER 17 –

•

ACTIVATION – PART III:
DEEPENING YOUR CONNECTION

*"You cannot enter the heart with
the mind. You must surrender to
the presence of God in the heart."*
– Kahan

This is the closing part of the course of the Violet Light. These two meditations work together as part of the activation. Beyond that, the global one can be done on its own. They are the third part of the activation and a meditation for the planet.

Like in the previous parts of the activation, surround yourself with a mystical atmosphere. Switch off or dim the light, light a candle and an incense stick. Put soft relaxing music. Switch off all the phones. Sit on a cushion comfortably with crossed legs by the candle or on a chair.

Activation meditation

- ♦ *Put your hands in the mudra of compassion: middle finger and thumb joined.*

- ♦ *Breathe deeply three times.*

- ♦ *Let the natural rhythm of your breathing take you inside.*

♦ *Let your inner state of serenity be your support – give yourself to it.*

♦ *Now visualize your closest spiritual figure. It can be Jesus or any other. If you do not relate to any, create your own idea of Universal Love in manifestation.*

♦ *See him or her before you.*

♦ *See his face clearly, his expression serene, peaceful... extremely loving and supportive.*

♦ *See the Violet Light coming out of his third eye to your third eye. Stay like this for five minutes.*

♦ *Now see a beam of Violet Light streaming forth from the center of his chest – heart chakra – to yours. At the same time keep your vision of the third eye. Ten minutes. Eyes closed.*

♦ *Hear the Violet Light saying inwardly: "With the eyes you will see the innocence, with the heart you will see the Truth."*

♦ *Hear it three times.*

♦ *Now, let the presence of your spiritual figure go, thanking him/her for bringing you the activation in this way and enter into the next meditation.*

GLOBAL PEACE MEDITATION
FOR THE PLANET

You can do this one individually or with a group at any time. In a group, a person should guide the meditation by reading it aloud for all. Don't rush through the steps. Allow some space between them.

Global meditation:

♦ *Breathe deeply three times. Fingers in the mudra of compassion: middle and thumb touching.*

♦ *We place our awareness in the heart. We go into this temple of light deeper and deeper.*

♦ *If you are doing this meditation independently of the book do this invocation: "From the sacred place of the heart we invoke God Source, Jesus, Saint Germain, Virgin of Guadalupe, all the Ascended Masters, Archangel Zadkiel and Archangel Michael, the Spiritual Hierarchy of the planet, the Galactic Federation of Light and the Violet Light, to be here with us to guide us in this meditation of peace and light for Mother Earth."*

♦ *We now see the Ray of Violet Light descending upon the center of the circle. We see it anchoring itself into the Earth.*

♦ *A ray of Violet Light descends on us, entering into our crown chakra and going down to enter the heart.*

♦ *It expands from all the hearts and beyond them, to unite all hearts in a circle of Violet Light.*

♦ *Within the central ray of Light, we see a pearl of Violet Light containing all the presence of God.*

♦ *Rays of light come out of the pearl and enter our hearts.*

♦ *Feel and receive Its power, love and peace.*

♦ *The Violet Light now expands itself from the center in all directions encompassing the circle.*

♦ *It continues expanding, encompassing the hall, the building, the city, the country, the continent…*

♦ *…the planet and all of humanity.*

- *We see the planet surrounded with Violet Light.*

- *We see the Violet Light embracing all human beings.*

- *We see a violet fire alive in the hearts of all humanity. Within the fire we see the violet pearl.*

- *From each heart a ray of Violet Light comes out to join all other hearts, creating the brotherhood of light of humanity for the Earth.*

- *We now see the Violet Light entering into the hearts of all the religious and political leaders of all countries, opening their hearts and consciousness to true service, love and peace.*

- *We see the Violet Light blessing all children, teenagers and adults upon the Earth.*

- *The Violet Platinum Light now surrounds the Earth and mankind, bringing the planet to a state of deep love and peace.*

- *The Violet Light intensely goes into all places of the Earth, lacking love and harmony to reestablish peace and unity.*

- *Stay there for ten minutes.*

- *Now slowly return.*

- *Leaving the Violet Light surrounding the planet, we come back with a part of that light.*

- *See how the Light concentrates on the continent, the country, the city, the house, the room.*

- *We see the Violet Light anchored in the center of the circle as before. Within it we become aware of the violet pearl.*

- *Through the rays of light connecting the violet pearl with our hearts, the pearl of Violet Light is absorbed into each heart, merging with us and with all of humanity.*

◆ *The Violet Light remains also in the center of the circle to permanently bless the Earth.*

◆ *Now breathe deeply three times becoming aware of your individual body, mind, spirit, feeling you remain united as part of all.*

Giving thanks

If you have reached the global meditation after the third part of the activation:

"I thank God as the Power Source of all life, the Violet Light, all Ascended Masters, Archangels of light, angels and the I Am Presence of my higher Luminous Self, for supporting and materializing this activation of the Violet Light I have received through this book."

If you have performed the global meditation independently:

"We thank God Source, Jesus, Saint Germain, Virgin of Guadalupe, all the Ascended Masters, Archangel Zadkiel and Archangel Michael, the Spiritual Hierarchy of the planet, the Galactic Federation of Light and the Violet Light, for being here with us to guide us in this meditation of peace and light for Mother Earth."

In both cases close with this offering:

"I/We offer all this light, Grace and blessings for the liberation and spiritual ascension of all humanity, all sentient beings and the planet."

– Amen.

PART IV

FINAL VISION

"All beings share the same
spark of life from God.
If we would all see that,
we would love each other."

– K a h a n

– CHAPTER 18 –

•

MAKING THE MOST OF LIFE

"Surrender is joy,
service a way of life."
– Kahan

To be in service, that is to live a life of service, is not helping the needy or assisting the elderly three hours a week. That is a compassionate act of service and should be done. To live a life of service is to serve the Universe wherever we are, at all times. This is to provide assistance to the process of consciousness developing before us at any moment. It means serving the unfolding of the process of consciousness in which we are involved and not impeding it or blocking it. To resist it would be to stand on the way. To serve it is to get out of the way. This is what makes life really work. You might be so involved with your own processes, so involved with your personal karma that you cannot be of real assistance to the unfolding process of the present, you only see your limited self-centered perception. But that is fine, it is taking most of your attention because it is the first thing you need to solve. The more we are free from our personal karma the more we are in service.

Eventually we reach the point in which we do not make decisions any more. We are just one with whatever happens and we act accordingly to what is needed in each situation. We have surrendered, given up our small will to accept completely the Will of God. This is when it all really starts for us. This is when we make the most of life. This has nothing to do with your decisions about going to buy food, planning your trips or deciding to go to work. We are talking here about your inner will, this happens inside of you. But as that scheme of the greater will of God unfolds for you, you will see that those small decisions of the daily life, become very clear and flow naturally in the best direction for you and your life.

The Violet Light produces a reduction of the personal Karma and an expansion of the light within, leaving us freer to enter the process of serving in the present. This is where the joy is and where the way to our fulfillment lies, so we must seek to increase our light to enter into serving the present if we want to move forward at all levels.

God speaks to you in the present all the time. You have to tune finely to hear His voice. So you do not need to plan your life, He develops it to perfection if you stand out of the way, without interfering. If you do that, you will know every moment the direction to go. Situations and people will come to you, so you do not need to worry about creating them. The perfect ones will come if you let Him do it all. It is as if your inner voice has been activated, and you finally hear it.

THE TRUTH ABOUT SURRENDER

> *"As the Master surrenders to God,*
> *he accesses all His power."*
> – Kahan

The whole idea of surrender may make you feel uncomfortable. Looking at the quote may be puzzling, as surrender may be seen as an act where you are left powerless: at the mercy of an external force. Looking at it closer and deeper, you can acquire another perspective. What you surrender are your limitations, the limited identity with its toys: suffering, worry, fear, small will, in a word, your limited power. What happens then is that you open the door to the biggest power: your unlimited identity. This is in your Divine Self. True power is spiritual power. The other power is really nothing. To surrender is to change one for the other. The world of ego is unenlightened free will, a world of limited choices, a world unfulfilled. In surrendering you are empowered. You have an option in life: to use the power of ego or the power of God. It is in God we are invulnerable. We have all the power there. Without Him we have no power, we are vulnerable. This is important to consider. It is a completely different life you will live with one or with the other.

When we talk about surrender we mean let the ego go, embrace God. This implies embracing His power. This lies for us in the Higher Self. This metamorphosis has to be undergone at one time or another. You can work with ego power until you get tired of it and of its limits, frustrated at its limiting condition… ill, lonely, old, powerless. That is the end of the road for ego power. Then you might want to embrace God's power. This is the true resurrection: the promise of eternal life. What Christ embodies. Embracing God in us is embracing our Christ nature: I Am, Atman, Higher Self, Brahma, Tao. They are all the same. The only free choice a man can make is to surrender to God or not. Any other choice is not free; it is ego driven. If you surrender to God you are free. If you don't, any other choice is conditioned, therefore your will is not free.

To surrender does not mean you are weak, devoid of power. It means you are empowered by the power of life. So it is quite the opposite, you access a greater power. Such an act requires great inner mastery and therefore strength. In this great act you are sharing the power of that force we call "God" that empowers everything. All power is God's power. Even the small power you use in your life comes from Him. So why don't you surrender and open up to all of it. It is there for you.

•

– CHAPTER 19 –

•

ILLUMINATION FOR ALL

> *"So who then may be saved?"*
> *"With man it is impossible. But*
> *with God everything is possible."*
> – The Apostles and Jesus

We are coming out of a phase in the history of Humanity in which Man has believed that he had to suffer. Man believed he had to make a dying effort in order to achieve anything, because Man has believed God had abandoned him. He has believed it, and thus has lived it. He has believed in a hard God, not in a loving one and thus has lived it. In order to start seeing the true God, which is most loving and benevolent, you need to open up, let your old believes of God go. Then let Him show you what He truly is.

"God is for you what you believe Him to be."

Fatality does not exist. There is always the side of light and the side of darkness. You choose which one to look at. But now things are changing slightly. Until now Man's pursuit has been the evasion of his shadow: his dark side. Now it is the light that is following Man. Due to the high vibration of the energies upon the planet, the light within everyone is awakening. The light is chasing all our shadows inside to bring them to the light. We cannot sleep any more unconscious or immersed in our own darkness, because our light will come and wake us up. Light is not negotiating any more with our own darkness, it is chasing it until it is completely redeemed in the light. So there is no break for us now. We have no option: the choice is to be in the light or to be in the light – that's all. It is the commitment of God to all His sons, because of which He cannot see or allow any human being to be in the dark any longer. This is because of His love for us. That is the kind of God we have. This happens through our "I Am" presence being activated. This is true illumination, a state of awareness in which our shadows have been removed leaving us free to see and experience joy; suffering is finally gone as the inner shadows brought to the light have disappeared. There is no greater will for us than the Will of God. Then we realize joy is our right because it is the Will of God for us all. We understand that there is no way we can conceive or imagine anything greater than that, because if this was be so, He would have created it already. So we stand in awe in the middle of ourselves and of our lives, abandoning ourselves completely to that power, greatness and love, seeing God truly for the first time.

God has stood firmly inside every human being and He is not going away until we recognize Him. Then He is here to stay. If you are not in the light, you are suffering. The light dissolves all that which is not like itself: darkness. In resisting light we create suffering for ourselves since the power of that light is stronger than us. We'd better go along with it. We cannot resist the Will of God. God wants now every human being in the light. So we are entering into an era of no Karma, an era of Dharma, of light.

COSMIC LAUNDRY

I have heard that when we leave this world, if it is necessary for our evolution, we pass through regions of Violet Light for our own purification. This seems very reasonable to me having seen the powerful cleaning effect of the Violet Light. Isn't it fabulous then that we now can have all the potency of the Violet Light in this life? We can do an incredible work of Karma liberation and purification, to advance quantum leaps in our spiritual evolution in this life, accelerating our process and saving ourselves a lot of delays after life, so that we can go straight to regions of higher awareness, light and experience of God. In that sense, the Violet Light can be considered the "Cosmic Laundry." It is a special one since due to its characteristics it has only one program: "spin," and two speeds: "fast" and "immediate." Because this is the way it works. Such is its extremely high vibration. It is like the laundry service of God that cleans your karmic weight, cleans the obscurity you bring with you, leaving you with a new vibration, one which is very bright indeed. A great cleaning. It is necessary to have this service of cosmic laundry. It is in this way that we get ready for the jump to the new level. It is here and in this way that God exercises His greater power of Mercy, saving us from all our ghosts and evils. All those patterns that stop us from being as God created us.

It is as if we said:

"*Beloved Divine Power redeem me from my madness. Reestablish the Divine in me.*"

This is divine forgiveness. That is why you have to go through the cosmic laundry – "the karmic laundry." It cleans you and leaves you with a superior vibration. Remember that in low vibration waters are infested with terrible species: fear, anger, jealousy, resentment, hatred, doubt and the like. It is necessary to elevate our vibration to access the Luminous Self: our inner light. To elevate a balloon the weights have to be released. You don't rise to thousand feet with them. It is an impossibility. You have to be lighter. This is the same. To rise to the realms of spirit, to the bliss of the high regions, the heavy karmic weight has to be released. With negative karmas you have a terrible vision of the world: one of fear and limitation. From there you live a play of attack and defense.

When the Violet Light acts in you, it releases the chains in your heart, those that chain your vision to one of limitation and misery. In redeeming the past, it allows you to be fully in the love of the present. If you are carrying the burden of the past you cannot issue a response of love in the present. You are absorbed by the pain that generates a judging attitude and you don't see the reality before you. When you are in the present you are in love, because in the present there is only

209

love in you. The heart has to be restored to the experience of joy. That is the reality of our consciousness.

Let's see where we finally end up with this process...

PERSONAL MYTH: RESURRECTION

> *"Search life where life is, there where it never dies. Only that is the true life. Only in Him. Nothing else has life. He is the Source of life. He is the Resurrection and the Life."*
> – Jesus and The Ascended Masters

The goal in life is to achieve the personal myth. This is represented for a collective society, by the figure of an individual who has realized his own personal myth. This is the case with Jesus, Buddha and others. This figure represents the realization of all the divine potential that can be embraced, and it stands as a beacon of light for that civilization, the model to follow, the path to the goal.

In order to do the quantum leap that brings us completely into the Age of Light, we have to realize our personal myth. This is no more than to live our plenitude, to develop our potential, to enter into wholeness. We are not lacking anything, we just have to realize that we are complete. In that sense, what we lack is that realization. We can see in this light that the mythical quest for the Holy Grail, is really an inner voyage of discovery and realization towards the Source of eternal life, which cannot be other than the essence of the Christ in the depths of every man. Finding the Grail within and holding it with an awakened awareness, is the way to embody the personal myth.

Since Jesus the human being has not realized his personal myth. What has Man done in this evolutionary cycle that is closing now? He has given his power outside. Therefore he has never been able to realize himself. As Man gives away his power he makes it impossible for himself to realize his myth, then he starts to look for another way in which to live his life: He starts to create idols. Idols to adore and to which he grants power: the power he gave away. He has to find his power somewhere because he is not owning it, and therefore he has to create idols of power. Thus he is living in a way that fills the void left because love is lost, since love is the real power of Man. When he casts power away, love is gone with it.

Man has shut the door because he did not understand that love was really there, but it was covered with layers of pain. It was his work to remove the layers from his heart. Closing the door is the easy way out… but a way to nowhere, because without uncovering the love in the heart there is no love anywhere else. Life then becomes a hell in which man has fallen and in that agony, there is no possibility for him to realize the personal myth.

> *"Love is the only protection in a world of illusion."*
> – The Ascended Masters

This means love is the only safe place. Illusion is treacherous. Hence all human beings that have not moved away from illusion, live a deceitful life going around in circles looking at the reference of the personal myth, but never being able to come anywhere near it. It then becomes an unreachable ideal which state of grace is only for the mythical figure, when Jesus clearly said: "All I have done and more you will be capable of." In this state of affairs nobody understands any more what it is all about, because this planet and this Humanity as they are, do not make any sense. It does not work because we are not doing the race of love which is the only one that works and makes any sense, the only one that arrives somewhere worthwhile, the one that solves everything: life, searching and meaning.

Simply put: the quantum leap to the Age of Aquarius is to elevate the vibration of love of Humanity. This produces the recovering of the personal power and love allowing mankind to realize its personal myth, individually and collectively. This is what the Violet Light can do. Since Karma means living outside love, in order for Man to realize his personal myth he has to get rid of his karma and enter into love. When the fountain of love is alive in us, love comes out of us.

Love is not an act – something we do in a given moment. It is a state of consciousness, a way of living. This is when we are outside Karma. That spring of love inside each one has to be alive and flowing, without the restrictions that limit, as negative emotions, the natural loving state of a clean heart: the state from which the personal myth can be realized.

"The awakening to the inner light fully, takes Man to the Myth."

This process is the coronation of the human being, in which he connects from his seventh chakra on the top of the head, with the Divine. Only then is man complete. The superior chakras become fully awakened and Man acquires divine consciousness, realizing the Myth. From there he truly loves. Obviously when the Myth is realized it is not a myth any more, it is a reality. The top chakras are closed because of guilt and weak faith. We have to convert to our higher reality, the luminous one, which is the way to return to our impeccability: our guiltless state of being.

The Violet Light brings the spirit of the Messiah for humanity to help it realize its personal myth in a global way. It is a death and a resurrection. The man from Aquarius is reborn from the ashes of the old man, as a new ascended being. It is a metamorphosis. In this process we collapse, we fall apart. We have to look at what has fallen and understand there is nothing to be recovered, we have to let go to the old form to embrace the new one greater and more luminous. What has collapsed will not get up any more. It has died. What comes along is a new birth a being with more consciousness. It is not a matter of picking up what has fallen down, it has to do with being reborn in a new way. The illusion collapses giving rise to a new being. This is the process of transition in which we all are. The perfect mantra for this is:

"I am the Resurrection and the Life"

We should all use it to activate the vibration of our myth.

Divine Energy activates the myth

There is an essential issue in all this: all the mythical figures have arrived at their realization through the contact or communion with a higher state of energy. We call that energy: "Grace." It is the same as saying The Holy Spirit or any other equivalent definition. The presence of The Holy Spirit is what all the mythical figures encountered in their intense spiritual quest, as they reached for the knowledge and experience of God. They activated through The Holy Spirit their inner light. And as we have seen to have the inner light activated is absolutely essential. This is what the mythical figure has done. But it has only been possible through an injection of divine energy. Their spiritual effort took them there. That effort provided the opening of the gate to Grace. Now, that Grace comes to reunite Man with his Divine Creator. Man enters finally into communion with the Holy Grail: the place of God, the gate to all mysteries.

We know the original purpose of religion was to reunite Man with God. But from a conversion towards his interior, within the sphere of his Inner Self which is where he reunites with the Divine. But... if we make man believe since he is a child that God is not inside... we make him dependent on the outside – and of its representations of Him – where he will look to have that reunion, thus impeding him the realization of his myth. In that way many spiritual institutions have provided a great disservice to the evolution of mankind, assuring as much as possible that this mythical realization did not happen, as this would have thrown them off power and produced their dismantling. By definition if humanity has not realized its personal myth it is dependent upon external forces and powers. God is not considered a external force because He is within Man.

Man has not had global access to a source of spiritual energy that could provide for him that leap, and the institutions which he has trusted to guide him have not offered him that in a true sense. So Man has not taken the jump to his higher consciousness with the energies available – until now. All in life depends on the energy inside. And that energy is the one that needs to be activated for the myth to realize itself in everyone.

Inevitably mankind has to move on to the consciousness of the humanity of Aquarius, if not we do not culminate this era. Man has to realize his personal myth because he is divine seed. Realizing it, is to realize his divine mission. The personal myth of the man of this age is called: "The Age of Aquarius."

The winged serpent

We saw earlier that in Mayan culture the mythical figure is "Kukulcan," the winged serpent. They considered the winged being the realization of the personal myth: a being that ascends. For the Aztecs this happened by the eagle holding the serpent. Those of the eagle are the wings the serpent develops, those of the higher being. The serpent – lower self – is overpowered by the eagle – higher self – and is consumed by it. The difference in perspective is huge: one looks at life from the ground; the other sees all from the sky. This is a transmutation of the lower being into the higher being: consciousness ascends from the serpent to the eagle.

To the ordinary human being – the serpent – wings are developed, undoubtedly through contact with the Divine, becoming the myth: he ascends to his divine being. This is a divine transmutation, the highest transmutation possible. It activates Man's divine light and power, his immense divine love. In this way he is able to fly – rise up – above and beyond ordinary existence. Here, in the pass to the Age of Aquarius is where we develop wings... we ascend.

– CHAPTER 20 –

•

ABOUT GOD

"Life is joy. The moment we move away from joy, we move away from God."
– Kahan

GOD IS A HUGE PIE

God is a huge pie that you can have complete. If you have not taken the whole of it, it means you are cutting small pieces of it and think this is enough for you. You feel that is what you deserve: a small bit of it. Most people are lacking something in them and in their lives, because they have not taken all God has for them. They are starving but the cake is sitting there. What happens is that we have created a valve that regulates the connection with Him, and we control how much of the infinite gets through the pipe that supplies us. We have the control and we filter what enters from this divine current to our lives. This is the amount of faith we have.

You open the valve just a little because you are afraid, because you don't believe, or you open it completely and receive all the gifts from God. The best option is to throw away the valve... it is your fear. The Violet Light is a way of getting rid of the valve and have the entire pipe directly connected to God, with all its potency.

God gives you all. He gives you all the cake to start with... and asks you: "How much of it do you want?" He gives you all the power. There you have it all. You decide. With your faith or lack of it, you go along cutting pieces of the pie. So you are the one cutting God…What size? What measure? What abundance?

How much of the cake do you want?

God let's you play your game as you want. You play to believe in the god you want. He considers you equal to Him: God. So you play to be the God you want to be: a mediocre being full of lacks; a complete being healed, perfect… this is what you will create of yourself. The option to see yourself equally perfect as Him, is fully yours. You either decline or you take it. You take all the pie, or you don't. He provides the power for you to realize your vision: a perfect one or an imperfect one. Thus you will live the reality you have created for yourself from this vision. You have the whole pie for yourself. The fact that you don't eat it doesn't feed others, it does not add anything to anyone. It only starves you. If you eat it, this doesn't make anyone suffer from starvation. Each one has a complete pie, the divine pie. God has not given more to some than to others. What each one has done with that pie is everyone's own responsibility.

You have to restore that knowledge, that consciousness that God is the endless supply of all in your life. He is the supply of your power. When this is understood idols of power are not needed. Thus we stop seeking them to get from them what we are not getting from God. The power they pretended to have was never real. That is why we are all continually let down by them. Until we all return to God and understand what He means for us inside, as the key to our existence and our abundance, we will not be happy or at peace; we will not be healed or perfect; we will be in any sort of lack. We must all eat our pie.

BECOMING FREE

"God has no structure."

The more you enter into communion with spiritual energy, the more your structures fall down. This is why almost everybody experiences periods of feeling lost, as they advance spiritually. This is good and it is a good sign: real progress is taking place. As a dear friend Marise said when we met in India, taken by surprise after being with Sai Baba for a Darshan: *"All my life I have seen myself as a strong woman. Now I am falling apart."*

The powerful spiritual energy that emanated from Sai Baba, was doing away with her rigid structures. As the wisdom of her comment shows, she wasn't strong in real terms, she perceived herself that way. The beauty of her comment lies in her humility: she accepted the fact. It was happening, she was being transformed. That non-resistance allowed her to stay serene in the midst of her structures collapsing. It also kept her open and receptive to a greater experience of her own divinity.

So avoid the contraction from a fearful reaction, when this is the case for you. Take heart in the fact that keeping up those structures is accepting death, the death that being half alive means: decadence due to crystallization. Crystallization is the state of not flowing because of fear of the future, therefore one holds on to the way things were in the past, and in trying to bring them to the present, becomes solidified with structures. That is the meaning of "becoming statues of salt" if they looked back at the burning city they were leaving, from the famous passage of the Bible. Statues of salt are crystallized beings, dead with structures from looking at the past. Those structures do not allow greater light and love power into you. The sooner they fall, the less upset you will experience. As you become free of limiting structures, you experience freedom. Light enters and structures dissolve. So as you get nearer and nearer to God Consciousness in you, you will be less structured and more loving. When you are in love, you don't need structures:

"The structure of God is light.
The structure of God is love."

Where there is love there is no need for structures. Love dictates and organizes all in the most perfect way, all the time. Love is such a high vibration that structures cannot form. They do not have time to set. So as your structures melt and give way to space in you, you will work more and more from love. There you do not need to hold on to any structure, love itself is your reference and your guide. Where there is love, you don't need a reference. Love is your reference. You do not need a reference on how to act, love is your reference all the time. You will find in it all the power and wisdom you need.

God is so active in these times that whatever is not good for us, will be challenged and changed. It is this that brings a breaking down of structures and hence freedom. You need to understand this: holding on to a sinking boat does not make any sense. Our collapsing structures are like a sinking boat that we need to let go. It is not for us to look at the past, that which is gone. Our mission is to look forward at what is coming anew to replace the old. Then to embrace it all together to create a new reality of unity and light.

God is looking after us all the time to help us. But our egos are so familiar with what doesn't work, that think it is natural. It has never been so crazy. We need to understand that everything that comes to our lives is a blessing from God. He is bringing what we all need. The result is up to us. What do we do with it? We can make a mess of it, or we can rise above the lower spheres. Let's remember that we are creators. God did not create the madness in the World. We did. He has given us a beautiful planet, wonderful bodies, great energy...what do we do with them?

I have people coming to my conferences that say: *"God is everything, light, darkness... the good things, the bad things..."* This is a dangerous misconception too abundant in these confusing times.

God Is. And what He is, is Light.

He is One. So that Light does not cast a shadow. There is no darkness in God. How can you have all the light, be Oneness, and have a dark side? It is impossible. That is separation, not oneness. The light and dark they are referring to, happen once you get down here. Here, there is separation. Our ego blocks the light, then we create darkness. But let's not confuse our own shadow with a creation from God. We have to realize we are "on the way" blocking the light. When we block God, we have darkness. It is not in Him.

PEACE HAS A PRICE

If you want peace, be ready for it. Be ready to be faced with what is not peace in you. Ready to accept that, in many ways, you are not walking ways that create peace and to be prepared to change them for ways of peace. Remember, when you ask for peace everything in your life may fall down. Everything that is a lie in you will be shaken. Because all the things that are not peace in you, are structured in a way that cannot hold peace. They have to be rearranged in order to be aligned with the vibration and consciousness of peace. These things do not hold peace because they hold deceit. That is where all the suffering and pain you experience comes from. You want to get into a new state of things as fast as you can. Then everything will be realigned, but then you need to recognize you are being helped. Since you have asked for peace, everything that is not peace has to be removed from you, or transmuted into light. If you want to evolve this is necessary... but remember it when you are in the midst of it. Essentially we are not at peace because in many areas of ourselves we are less than love, we haven't embraced love there. We need to understand this and move towards its resolution.

We all want to become free. But too often we are not prepared to pay the price for it; nor to assume what it means. We cannot have the same old ways and structures and become new. We cannot embrace the new if we don't let go to what is causing us pain. Great part of what has stopped mankind individually and collectively in moving forward, is precisely this. We need to mature. We need to understand that every day we can create the reality, the world in a new way through letting go, forgiving the past in all the multidimensional ways in which we can forgive. This is essentially, as A Course in Miracles says, letting go of the wrong vision. Otherwise we are bringing the same thing with us to the future, and it all looks the same. So let's all jump into the cosmic ship of high vibration that will help us infinitely in releasing the old world, because a world and a life of love and peace starts with you and I, right here right now. So let's find the high vibration of love power of the soul and live from there. Then we can create a Luminous World.

PART V

THE VIOLET LIGHT EXPERIENCES

*"The reencounter of one's heart
with God, is everybody's
deep yearning. To feel supported
by this mighty presence of love and
power, is the only way to exist in
sanity and plenitude."*

– K a h a n

THE STORIES OF PEOPLE
TOUCHED BY THE VIOLET LIGHT

"Where there is no love
there is ego. Where there
is love, God is present."
— Kahan

I want to share with you a gem, or rather a cluster of them that like a constellation of stars, shines in the Heavens of the Violet Light to illumine us all, filling us with awe, wonder and gratitude. It is a selection of stories from people who have received the activation of the Violet Light over the years in the live courses, and reported what was happening to them during and after. Their spirit shines in my heart. I offer you humbly this greatness from the touch of God in the hearts and lives of our brothers and sisters of this Earth, so that their experiences also shine in your heart. I hope it serves to illuminate and bless the life of all.

INNER REENCOUNTER

Hello Paco,

I am Nathaly a member of the initiation course of the Violet Light. The truth is that only six days have gone by since the course, and I feel marvelously well. This reencounter with my heart, with God has been and it is the best thing that has happened to me. I know this is only the beginning. I am anxious and very emotional about continuing on this new path of peace and love. Please write to me, I want to keep in touch with you and with all the group of Violet Light in Cancun.

Nathalie G.

THE INFLUENCE OF THE LIGHT

Dear Paco,

I took the course of the Violet Light last Saturday, and from that afternoon I started to perceive clearly the wonderful influence of this divine light. I am completely certain that I didn't choose to assist to this course, but that I was really called to the light by our brother Jesus. I prefer not to talk of the experiences I lived since I desire to treasure them in the depth of my being, and again I want to thank you for the time you took in teaching us to walk in the light. It has been amazing to realize again these days, that unfortunately I was educated in a society and a religion that made me think that I do not deserve to share divinity, that we do not deserve happiness, or to be well, that life has to be a terrible fight even against oneself, and that this is the only way to achieve anything – not to mention happiness, that is something simply unreachable. I would like you to recommend to me some books that strengthen the idea that we are deservers of the light in our own right. Many thanks again, I hope we will see each other on the 11 and 12 December in the second level of the course. I would like your comments on what I write today. I send you a strong hug.

Alfredo

At the beginning of that second course, we all shared our experiences of the previous course. Alfredo said to all of us:

"This could have been one of the most difficult periods of my life. But it has not thanks to the Violet Light. I feel supported from above."

Alfredo at the time was a director in the banking industry.

CHANGE OF PERSPECTIVE

Dear Paco,

I want to thank you Paco for the event of allowing me with your teachings to find the way to my inner universe. This has allowed me to understand life with another perspective and to consciously begin an emotional growth, that has been translated into seeing the marvels that daily and at every hour, God gives us as a gift and that in our selfishness many times, we don't allow ourselves to see them.

Rogelio A.

BREAKTHROUGH

A lovely man called Joaquim came to the course in a small village in Spain. Right from the start, he felt somewhat negative about certain things. At one point before lunch, he asked a very intellectual question. I explained to him that he should not worry about that, and that it all would become clear soon. But he tensed and did not let go of his concern. At lunchtime, the group walked to a restaurant and I approached him to see how he was.

I had a very unwelcoming reception from him in which he clearly expressed he was not enjoying the course, including the fact that I was not answering his questions. After trying to reach out to him, I saw there was no way through that negativity at the time, so I let things take their course. I had the feeling inside me that everything was fine. In the afternoon session he asked something with a noticeably different attitude – he was more positive, his expression was different. At the end of the course he came up to me in all the movement that usually takes place then, and shaking my hand intently thanked me for the course.

Two weeks later he phoned me… *"First I want to apologize for my attitude in the course… I found it unsettling you would not answer my questions… I am very well, things are happening… I am changing with the Violet Light… You were right in all you said."* Then he asked for my advice on some issues and how to apply the Violet Light to them… and said he was ready to take the next level of the Violet Light. He called me about every two weeks for a month or so. In one of those calls, he said that he wanted to take The Violet Light Workshop – the second course – soon and that the rest of the group did not seem so anxious about it.

COMMENTS FROM PEOPLE

"The Violet Light is so simple to be with. It is a space of great peace to be in. It does to you with its intelligence – you don't have to do."
Lila Lopez. Executive. California.

"I go on working with the Violet Light and it does me a lot of good, it fills me with peace, better said: with a lot of peace, it is incredible and it works. I want to thank you for all that you do. Thank you for being there!"
T.B. Spain.

"I think everything is fabulous because I am working with The Violet Light."
Valery Badgget. Business Developer. California.

"I congratulate you for all you have done with The Violet Light, and for what you are doing to facilitate and produce the entering of the millennium of light, peace and love that we all want for our beloved planet."
Guillermo Sanchez. Meditation instructor. Chopra system.

"The Violet Light Grace is the only way to get rid of misqualified energy."
David Lawrence. Diplomat. US.

"Soon after the Violet Light course, I confronted a situation that would normally make me very angry. This time it didn't. I felt my personality had changed."
Josune O. Nurse. Spain.

"Today I have had a rebirth."
Course participant. Spain.

"I have received so much tenderness and compassion at the beginning that I have not said anything in all the course."
Course participant. Spain.

HARMONY FOR ALL

A company owner commented the night after the activation with the Violet Light, that his Meditation practice with the light had been very different – very deep – and he was going to practice it every day. A friend of his, a very successful doctor, reported feeling very harmonized. A woman who took the activation course with them, said a few days later that she was radiant. In the bus she took to work, she felt the atmosphere became harmonized with the Violet Light. She found using the Violet Light at work, that the children she had in therapy became calmed. She said she was meditating with the Violet Light as she learned in the course.

EXPERIENCES OF THE VIOLET LIGHT BASE COURSE

"In the course of the Violet Light, within the sound of silence I felt the mercy of Creation, of love expressed as light."
Beatriz Alvarez Ferriz.- Communication executive.

"This course is like three years of psychotherapy."
M.T. Housewife.

"I saw Jesus descending upon the place without touching the floor, with his tunic radiating golden light."
S.P. Independent worker.

"After the course of the Violet Light I feel power in me."
A.M. Business owner.

"I worked with the Violet Light before, but it wasn't like this. Things dissolve out into nothing. The Violet Light unpacks me."
Valerie Badgett. Business Developer. California.

"With the Violet Light things move immediately into the direction they need to go."
Lila Lopez. Executive. California.

"I had the vision of Jesus in the center of the group, and in the final meditation the Universe was in the center of the circle."
I.T. Student.

*In the middle of the course: **"I never see anything in meditation. But I have just seen a ball of violet fire that entered me."*** At the end of the course: ***"I don't want to talk because of the ecstasy."***
Course participant.

"After the course of Violet Light I was in such peace and in a very elevated mystical state."
L.C. Accountant. Mexico.

"There was a lot of light. I saw myself surrounded with Violet Light. Before I could not see it."
Daisy Ponce. Real State.

"I saw before me like a prism of Violet Light. I experienced a lot of peace."
Martha Torres. Art teacher.

"I feel as if I have gone to a gas station and have been filled up (with high octane)."
Course participant.

"I have never taken a course like this. In it, I have felt the presence of God."
L.A. Cooking instructor.

●

Even though these wonderful people express their gratitude to me for what happened, I take no merits at all for this. The work I do is in the hands of the Ascended Masters and what happens, is the effect of the Violet Light. It is the power of God which does it all.

EXPERIENCES IN THE VIOLET LIGHT TRANSMUTATION WORKSHOP

"The temple of the Violet Light… for me it was to arrive at a place I already knew."
S.L. Executive.

"A cascade of Violet Light was coming down and it enveloped me. I disintegrated and started to ascend in the Violet Ray of Light. I was light. I ascended through the light and became the whole Universe. After a while I became integrated again and came back to manifest as an individuality."
J.C. Company owner.

"In the temple of the Violet Light there were Masters in reverence to this light. I was part of the light. The Masters invested me with the same light. I saw the temple before it was mentioned, and I saw it exactly as it was described. Afterwards I went to an impressive sea of peace. There were whales working for us and they said that there is a lot of hope for our planet: "There are many helpers. We will make it, and like that sea the planet would be." They said. I heard the sound of the Universe."
Ana B. Therapist.

"Now in the second course of Violet Light, I see the faces of the people who took the first course with me, and they are changed within and without. I see serenity in people that did not have it"
Jose de Jesus G. Restaurant owner.

"In level "I" of the Violet Light, I had an encounter with my spiritual Master who revealed to me who he was (one of the archangels). He confirmed to me my mission in this life. I was crying at the time, and I feel very moved."
A. M. Business owner.

"I felt love, peace, tenderness, compassion, power. The light brought me all these, and it turned into all I wanted. It ordained everything to perfection. I asked her: How can I serve you? "First it is you. Heal, cure yourself to be able to give. Do not worry." It radiated light to me. I received a bath of energy. It was a gift of integration for me."
M.E. Director of meditation center.

"To become aware of my wounds and to live them day by day under the shelter of the Violet Light, has made me extremely conscious that I have a brilliant life ahead of me. I think it is necessary to go through all this to realize that I by myself, will not be able to move out of it without the presence of the light in my life."
Alfredo Magana. Banking Executive.

BEYOND DEATH

In the Violet Light Transmutation Workshop there is a practice to transmute the moment of death, in which we travel to that future event with the help of the Violet Light. Often the experience people have of this event is one of peace and harmony. They see themselves as a being of light that leaves the body behind and moves on his journey towards the Universal Light. Often they are accompanied by their own spiritual Masters and move within a space filled with light. They feel very expanded, beyond limits, and there is no fear or concern. The whole experience of moving beyond this plane is very natural. They tend to reach regions of light, expansion and peace. One of the most common aspects of the experience is the encounter with The Light, as God. Death is seen in a different way, and most of the fear and uncertainty about it is gone.

PAST LIVES

Another experience of the Violet Light Transmutation Workshop, is a practice in which we travel to past lives. The purpose of this is to resolve and liberate any karmas or issues, that might be affecting us in this present life. The powerful loving presence of the Violet Light there, allows us to go on this journey. Most people have visions of previous lives and have experiences of them. The Light and the process allow them to release energy and emotions that were blocked at the time of the experience. This opens up a vision of our past life experience, and allows people to see beyond the mental frame that considers only this life as real, without taking into account anything before or after it. The liberation provided by this practice produces a very positive effect in this present life.

MESSAGES

A woman called me on the phone the Thursday after the course, to tell me her story. The course had been on the previous Saturday. We were on the phone for half an hour. This is the extract of it:

"My Mother in Law called me after six months, as if nothing had happened. For years we have not been in good terms. My children and my husband laughed for the first time and did not argue. They never laugh. They are always in conflict. We all feel in a bad mood often. It has always been like that. Nobody ever smiles. After years of desperation I tried everything, techniques, systems, nothing worked. I went to another country three times to do some rituals. I didn't know the smile of my children. This is a miracle... a whole family. Now there is harmony and laughter in my family. Thank you for appearing in my life."

She was so moved by this that she wanted to call me straight away to thank me. I still remember the relief in her as she could not believe finally she could hear her family laugh. I was astounded at her story and at the effect the light was having in her family.

A long time after she took the Violet Light course, a woman sent me this message:

"I have received your messages always motivating us to continue in love and putting away fear. Sincerely you sowed a vision and a very special way of life in the power of the Violet Light."
I.S. Course participant.

LETTERS

A LOVING HEART

"First of all I want to tell you that it has been a gift to meet you. I am delighted to know that there are people in this world like you. I took the first level of the Violet Light in November 2001. It was a beautiful experience difficult to explain. This course has been crucial in my life. From the moment it started, I felt the vibrations of the Violet Light. I traveled inside myself and I was upturned but for the better. The changes in my life and in the way I feel, have been manifesting a progressive improvement. I have a neighbor who became very ill. When she was taken to hospital, I followed her. She was put in a section with oxygen assistance and a drip. I entered to say good-bye to her. I gave her a kiss and talked to her. She did not answer; she was leaving. I said to her that if she went, she would go with the light, but if she decided to stay she was very welcomed. I left. In leaving, I started to pray for her and when I arrived home, I did a meditation and I invoked the Violet Light. I asked that she would be helped. Next day she was the same very ill but she didn't die, instead she was getting better. Some days latter I visited her. I said hello to her and I was surprised to see how she reacted when she saw me. She moved

233

her arm towards me and held my hand, and called me as she always did. Her glance and her manner were very tender. Today she continues at home with an oxygen supply, but she is well. It seems that is not the time for her. Impressive. Well I hope I have portrayed part of what faith and the Violet Light can do. To tell you the truth it scares me a bit, its power, its strength. Well Paco, forever yours.

Someone who appreciates you sincerely."

Carmen

Carmen's friend finally passed away a few months later. We are both very happy to know that she was blessed in her life by the Violet Light in God's Will. Carmen has worked as a surgery nurse for more than 14 years in the North of Spain. She has three children.

TRUSTING THE LIGHT VISIONS

Hello Paco,

"I am going to tell you a story. On the beach called "wild," there was a sunset on the sea, very beautiful. I was with a friend and we addressed the sun before parting to say farewell. I thanked the sun. When we turned around I saw an intense violet color that was very evident in all I could see; violet stood out from everything else, there were many violet things: towels, clothes, the bar screen, the people going up the hill appeared in violet clothes. The hues in general were very special and I felt that the sun had feelings, and that it was very happy. My friend saw all this too (he has not even taken the course of the Violet Light) He said: "This is because we looked at the sun." I said, "yes." In another conversation, we mentioned that event on the beach. He said again that the event should have some explanation, possibly it was because we had been looking at the sun. I told him to

leave scientific explanations to the scientists and to stay with what he saw. I wanted to share this with you. Receive a hug with my love."

Begonia Sarmiento

Begonia has worked for the local government, in one of the north regions of Spain for more than 20 years.

THE VIOLET LIGHT IN ACTION

OPENING OF THE HEART

Martha Del Villar told me this story before taking the Master Course of the Violet Light.

"I work with a person I find very hard in our working interactions. I asked for her, I prayed. One day I saw with my eyes a ray of Violet Light above her, and her face was illumined with the Violet Light. In the following days this person started to turn soft, sweet. Even to the point of admitting she was feeling very sensitive."

EMOTIONAL REFINEMENT

One of the main aspects of this work is that the Violet Light brings purification and refinement to people. One example is that of Maria Jesus Azkue who after taking some of the courses, changed radically her diet and drinking habits, to the great surprise of her usual friends and I think to hers too. She started very conscious eating habits towards greater health and energy. As a result of her outer and inner changes, she changed physically and inwardly becoming much more radiant. She said on many occasions: *"Before I had to control my anger. After the Violet Light connection, I don't have to control it*

235

because it just does not happen as it did before. This has changed in me. I have found God inside me. Before I did not feel connected spiritually. I used to work things out with my mind. Now I let things flow and have gained effectiveness. I obtain better results with less effort."

The change in her personality expresses a refinement of the emotions, a process brought about by the positive effect of the Violet Light. This is very common in people after the connection with the Violet Light. The rest of her comments speak for themselves.

Maria Jesus is as to date the president and founder of the Biscayan Astrological Association of Spain.

AN AMAZING LIBERATION

A few days ago – it is now December 2002 – in one of my Tai Chi classes, a woman approached me to tell me something very surprising. Since I met her, I could feel that her aura had terrible energies and being near her was a very distressing experience, to the point of having to harmonize my aura intensely after being near her. When she approached me she said:

"Thank you. I know you have been sending me healing."

In fact, when I realized the state she was in, I sent her Violet Light and asked the Ascended Masters to help her intensely. I was very concerned about her and did not know what could help her. When I heard what she was saying about it, I thought it was truly amazing and my feeling of joy was immense.

"How can you say that?" I asked her.
"Because I know it was you." She answered.
She continued…*"One day I had to lie down in bed and I felt heat and cold through it. Afterwards I felt very well. Another day, more*

recently, I received Violet Light and Golden Light and I saw many colors."

Before this fabulous work of the Masters and the Grace of the Violet Light, I felt great awe. I had actually felt the energy of her aura different, a week after I had asked for blessings for her. To me this is a miracle. I was truly worried about her. I did not know how to help her or who could help her. I was concerned about the amount of time in terms of years, that it could take her to free herself from that condition... only about a month had gone by between me asking for blessings and she telling me this. That day I noticed her light had increased. She was lighter, happier and her eyes had a spark. Words were useless. I kept saying to myself: "Thank you, thank you, thank you, Violet Light, Ascended Masters..."

GIFT OF LIGHT

Laura wanted to tell me her surprising experience soon after the course of the Violet Light. When I spoke to her she was very much centered, positive and motivated for the opening and changes she felt the Violet Light was producing in her. This is an extract of what she shared.

"At the weekend I received a wonderful gift through you. I have already started to savor it, enjoy it and use it fully with the certainty that this gift is permanent; it is only up to me to know all its hues. Thank you so much again. In the final part of the activation in the course, I felt my body expanded like rubber, everything was being pulled and twisted inside, so to speak. Then like a huge rubber band it was released and it went back to its place at the speed of lighting. It was incredible for me because with this experience I know I have started a process of unblocking, something that did not want to let go, started to give in. Also the Violet Light started to appear everywhere I go."

RETURN TO THE LIGHT

This is the amazing story Marian wanted to share with all of you.

"Since I was a little girl, when I closed my eyes I saw colored lights that sometimes were accompanied by sounds. It was a melody that, although it was different from what I could identify as music, was very pleasant. I could often see some people with a white light around their body. When I asked my family about the meaning of my visions and perceptions, the answer I obtained was that it was the result of my imagination as a girl. Through time I wanted to convince myself that this was the case, but years went by and I was not a girl any more, and I continued seeing lights…

At one point in my life, I entered into a doubting phase. I started doubting everything. I ended up rejecting all spiritual things. I got rid of all my spiritual books. I didn't want to know anything about spirituality. My aunt was very involved with spiritual matters. When she passed away, in her funeral, I could sense peace and joy. I addressed her asking her, that if in reality there was something else I wanted proofs. I wanted to see to believe. And I went back to seeing auras and lights. Soon after I started to see a bright light of violet color when I closed my eyes.

Later on I met Paco Alarcon in a conference of the Violet Light and then after that, I met him personally through common friends. Then I told him I had been seeing inside, for over a year, a violet light moving in circles. I asked him what this could be. He clearly answered: "What you see is The Self. It is Your Self. The Violet Light is divine light."

Months later, I took one of his courses. It was a true initiation for me. In the course I saw the Violet Light everywhere with my open eyes. It was in the air of the hall, on the carpet, in people's auras points of Violet Light were shining like stars. Our clothes had violet auras. I also saw it around the flowers on the main table. It was all a miracle being put in our hands. An energy of high frequency was arriving at

238

the place. The entire hall was surrounded by Violet Light. Everything was in it, except the personal things we left outside the hall. This was for me a confirmation that the light arrived there through Paco and through all of us. The things outside the room did not have light. After the course in my home for a couple of days, the Violet Light was still arriving. It was in my surroundings. It even reached the people that were with me.

After the course, I started sending Violet Light to people close to me and things started to shift for the better, in them and in my relationship with them. My life has changed in a number of ways, resulting in less influence of negative attitudes and a clear shift towards positive and loving attitudes. As a result I feel happier. The positive result of putting the Violet Light into daily situations is immediate and my life is lighter and easier to handle. But the amazing thing was to feel the immense transmuting power of the Violet Light in conflicts, in the difficult daily situations. The Violet Light has the immense power to change conflictive situations."

Marian

Marian works in a restaurant and looks after her two sons, in a small town in the North of Spain.

AFTER THE CONFERENCE

Before I give a course, I usually give a conference. In it, the whole overview of the Violet Light's role in this age upon the planet, is seen. The effects of the Violet Light and why it works the way it does, are explained. It is a true revelation of what is happening with the world and with humanity behind scenes. An eye-opener. There the presence of the Violet Light can be felt, those days before the course.

Purification of the heart

A woman called me the day after a conference feeling very sad. She had a deeply rooted emotional blockage that was being purified from her. She knew it. She was also feeling a great deal of energy in her heart with a lot of heat, when she practiced her own meditation. I explained to her how the Violet Light opened her channels and chakras during the conference and that something was being opened in her heart. Also I made clear how through this she was being freed of old negative emotions, blocking a fuller experience of love in her. She acknowledged this readily. She seemed to understand to a point the dynamics of energy, and admitted to having some unsolved emotional blockages related to her expression of love.

A vision of the Violet Light

A lady who left the conference room at an event in the Esoteric week of Colindres, Spain, because of an intense cough came to me at the end of the event. She told me she had gone outside, to the garden to get some fresh air. When walking back to the main building to rejoin the conference, she saw a dome of violet light above the conference hall that surrounded it. This was night time. She mentioned the hue was intense violet in the middle and lighter violet towards the edges. I thanked her for sharing this beautiful experience, and told her that the Ascended Masters and the Violet Ray of Light make their presence felt at the conferences, descending upon the place.

Many other experiences have been reported all to do with feeling intense energy or heat, having a sort of spiritual connection or experience. Many years ago at one point in the conference, a woman said that she was experiencing what was being said there at the energy level. All natural effects of the presence of the Violet Light.

MY OBSERVATIONS

I have witnessed and have been involved in so many events and experiences with the Violet Light, that I would need a separate book to tell all. Maybe I will do it. One interesting situation that shifted immediately with the light, was when I was about to start a television interview. The person conducting the well-known program had received the information about our subject well in advance. He was hesitant about the subject – the overall view of the Violet Light in the world – and did not know how to approach it. Ten minutes before going before the camera he still had doubts. He came to talk with me with a serious expression on his face, and said we would approach the subject in a specific manner, that he was obviously more comfortable with. I said we should do it the other way around, since in my experience it seemed to fit the development of the subject much better. He went away feeling unsure about this. I kept relaxed, put Violet Light into the situation and let go. Two minutes before going into the program, he came back quite cheerful and said: "We'll do it your way."

I have to say that not only the interview flowed in an amazing way, but that his approach and questions were of the most outstanding level and professionalism, as he is well known for. So we had a great time and we covered the subject thoroughly, touching all and many unexpected angles that came up, because of the great flow of energy that was taken place during the interview.

There are some common effects of the Violet Light I have seen people experiencing over the years. I can say that people enter into a very deep, quiet space in themselves which fills them with serenity. The atmosphere in the course is very sacred. At the end of it we don't want to leave it; it is so wonderful to be in. People become filled with light. Their expression changes; they go in with a look on their faces and come out with another, their eyes filled with light. Many issues become clear for people. It is like an inner-life revision.

241

The general report from people soon after the course is that things shift in their lives as they find a new alignment. They feel a new connection with life, inner and outer. Their relationships also shift towards a greater experience, or leave their lives if they are obsolete. They also report experiencing an acceleration in personal processes and work issues. I prefer not to give personal details because it can be misleading. What happened to someone in these shifts might not be what someone else needs. As for their inner life, they experience greater peace, greater freedom and many issues stop being a problem. They feel an improvement in their meditation, if they practiced it before, and a greater spiritual connection. They often say they are feeling more detached from problems, and find their lives flow better. They also seem to find a greater connection with God and with their inner selves. Often they experience greater resolution, power and love. I can tell you from my own experience that when I see them after a week or months after the course, they appear brighter, have more light and seem more carefree. They often look better and younger. I can see a definite shift inside; even the way they look out from their eyes has changed.

Many people have found a movement of energy often in the chakras. They may feel emotional release in the liberation of blocked emotional energy. Also even liberation of physical pain. Most talk of experiencing the presence of God in one way or another. People's life situations have shown a strong tendency to move, when blocked. For some this has meant finding a job, or a career change. Others have been able to stop their addictions. Many times there have been sudden improvements in relationships. I have found people very happy, some extremely grateful at the changes that seemed to happen without great effort on their parts. And especially happy for what they felt inside.

Many people found their true mission in life after the connection with the Violet Light. Others rearranged their lives which changed for the better as they embraced new ways, new realities or new paths. Many experienced deep healing from the physical level to the emotional and mental sides, as all their inner and outer energies were restructured in new and more appropriate ways. Most people accessed a new and greater experience of love, and found out what to live with a more open heart means. Most found a new experience of their own inner divine power in action, from which to create their lives. But what is more meaningful to me is the inner peace they experience. This is a comment they all invariably make. It is as if something has happened deep inside that has transformed them completely as human beings. They radiate peace, an energy of light emanates from them, they seem to have become "bigger" and in that way to encompass life in a greater way. That gives them a different placement in life as if something essential has gone into place, changing their inner workings. All these are effects of the expansion of the energy of the heart and of the development of their spiritual awareness.

●

My story

It all started in September 1997 when I went to have an aura reading with Thelma de Leon, in Mexico City. In the reading she asked me at one point: *"Who is your Spiritual Master?"* *"Jesus,"* I replied with some uncertainty since he was the main one, but I felt I had others as well. She then said that the connection of light in my aura was that of the path of Jesus, and that I should concentrate on Him and have less intermediaries.

I did just that... that evening. I sat in meditation and invoked the presence of Jesus. I told him I was ready for the highest, for his highest teaching. I saw his face... his presence with me... and he brought me the Violet Light.

When he appeared after I called him, I realized he brought a light with him that was violet. Then he gave me a number of instructions for my spiritual work. One of the first things he said was: *"Meditate as much as you can in my presence."* The day after, he told me that in my presence the transmutation of others would take place. Then violet and golden rays of light were coming out of my heart chakra. He told me all that was going to happen with the techniques I would receive. I started meditating from the first moment with him, in the way he was telling me. His presence was there in front of me very intensely every time. Violet Light was pouring out of him. The intensity of Grace and energy were phenomenal. The experience of meditation was all I could wish for: full of peace, love and ecstasy. Those experiences went on for about three weeks. And after they continued in different ways for months.

The second day he put his hands on top of my head, then with all his energy and heart he transmitted to me a healing and a transmutation for my aura. He healed me completely physically and energetically. He said that I could assimilate it and that my aura then became violet. He explained that I could put golden and violet light into my body, chakras, energy channels, aura and use these techniques to give spiritual advancement.

I meditated for hours every day, maybe three, more at times. The bliss of it was immense. He was always there with the Violet Light that emanated from him. At other times the light just fell on me from above. The states of deep peace which I entered are totally indescribable in words, but I can say: "unity beyond anything," "total stillness inside," "fusion with my whole being," and "peace unknown in this world." The spiritual energy of those meditations was intense, very, very intense. The place where I lived was charged, saturated with energy even when I left it more than a year later.

At the beginning Jesus said to me to concentrate on meditating for the following thirty days, and that my life was going to change. I was meditating in the nights receiving from him the Violet Light. There was great sanctity and I entered again a place I already knew, what is known as the "Great Void" inside. A region of total freedom, limitlessness, love, and peace beyond imagination. A space of consciousness full of pure ecstasy. There you feel the power, the presence of God so intensely it is almost scary.

One night I felt very blessed after receiving some messages from Jesus. I had a great lightness in all my being. He gave me some instructions for meditation. Then I felt existing beyond mind and body, beyond everything. At the time, very intensely, I had the consciousness that everything was Violet Light as the spiritual substance that made everything up. I felt immersed in a sea of blue-violet light. I had the consciousness that I was Violet Light. That everything is this Violet Light in essence – God's Consciousness – the purest, non-manifest state of consciousness.

As I moved around in Mexico City to do my daily activities, I felt the presence of Jesus with me most of the time. There was a clear communication between us. One day after explaining some things to me he said : *"A long, profound, and strong meditation makes all the difference."*

About two weeks after that, I heard in meditation that I had turned into a generator of Violet Light, and that the Violet Light emanated from me. Three weeks after our first encounter, Jesus said that the transformation had taken place, that I had been completely connected with the Violet Light. He explained that my being emanated Violet Light constantly and that anybody entering in contact with me was going to receive Violet Light. He also mentioned that the connection with the Light and with him was stabilized, and that I was connected with the Father, with the source of the Violet Light directly. He explained that I could project the light in the direction that I wanted, into situations and people, past, present, future, and added that the Violet Light is love, wisdom, power, transmutation and liberation. He said that my aura had been expanded. This is what he told me. I had not a clue at the time what it was all about. I did not know the real meaning of it all. But everything he said became true.

Something that started happening, as Jesus had said to me at one point, was that I would perceive certain energies. Soon after the initiation, I started to see manifestations of the Violet Light with my open eyes. Seeing energies or lights is something that had rarely happened in my life. For many years, I had the custom of offering candles and incense before my altar prior to meditation. It is a custom from India, something they do as an offering to Spiritual Masters or to representations of God. I have seen it being done before photographs of Masters in temples, in altars and in the shores of the Ganges, a sacred river to the Hindu people – a form of the god Shiva. Just about two weeks after the completion of my initiation, I offered the candle at night before my meditation, as usual. I had just come back from giving a weekend peace retreat, in which I took people into meditation with the Violet Light. I was charged with the energy. To my surprise, as I moved the candle for the offering I saw a violet light following the candle's flame in the air. It was like a violet flame. It was such an amazing sight that I stayed with the offering for a long time, watching this manifestation of the Violet Light. It was an impressive sight, beautiful and full of peace. This has happened constantly since then in different ways.

During the period I was receiving the initiation of the Violet Light from Jesus, I wrote everything that happened. At the end of those magical weeks I looked at all the written material. It was then when it dawned on me that I had in my hands a complete course of Violet

Light. The rest of the material arrived during the three following months that year, in meditations and in revelations at any time. Like the information on the chakras, which arrived while traveling on a bus in Mexico City's main and busiest avenue. So I had to manage to write all the information on that crowded place, as it was all coming down.

That year I had created a number of inner peace retreats, that I gave in a ranch I hired along the old road to Cuernavaca, less than an hour from Mexico City. A ranch lost in the forests that surround a place called "Tres Marias," the little village's name. I decided to include the essential meditations of the Violet Light as part of the program of the retreats. When we reached the part of the retreat assigned to the Violet Light, to my surprise people were having the same experience I had in my initiation. This was amazing and it made me think: "something big is going on here..." Something I was not totally aware of yet. What was and is happening since, is that the Ascended Masters and the Violet Light manifest themselves in the courses bringing this spiritual energy down, changing the energy of the place and of the people there. They charge the place with Divine Energy and give people the initiation. The light itself connects with people directly, as they receive an injection of Grace: a tremendous spiritual acceleration. As time went by all this was becoming clear to me.

To tell you the truth I had not the faintest idea what was going to happen, or what was happening to me at the time. I just felt great, infinitely blessed, filled with Divine Grace and so liberated and transformed. How could I even question what was going on; whatever it was, I didn't want it to stop... and it hasn't. When Jesus started bringing the Violet Light to me, I could not possibly imagine I was going to be able to do the same with other people through that Grace. It didn't even cross my mind. And even now, it amazes me all the time. The light is always there at the right time, I feel it coming down and it starts blessing everyone. In any case it is not me doing it, although I know my part in it. The course wrote itself and it was there in my hands before I realized it was happening. Jesus and the Masters knew it all along and gave me the time and the space to find it out for myself.

During all that time, I often felt the presence of very strong energy in me. My chakras, specially the top ones, shimmered with energy, they were like open doors of energy and light spinning to the highest rate. Since then it is the Violet Light who often reminds me of its presence, in a bright spark of light before my eyes, often as a point of light next to my body or to the person I am talking with. Or when it appears as an incredibly bright point of Violet Light floating in the air, that stays there for me to see it. The Divine Power that emanates from it and the consciousness that pulsates there, cannot be understood with the human mind. More recently it has appeared as the beautiful Violet Platinum Light, moving smoothly in the air as a serpentine of light.

At the time of the initiation even outside meditation, I felt enveloped with the Light. I remember a very special night for me in which I walked from the metro station to a friend's house. All the way I was immersed in an ocean of Violet Light. I felt ecstatic.

In January 1998 I decided to take out of the retreats the teaching of the Violet Light, and to structure all the knowledge that had arrived in an independent course. The Violet Light initiation course was born. There was so much material and information, practices and meditations, that one course was not enough. So Level II of the Violet Light was created. This is now called: "The Violet Light Transmutation Workshop." After a while the consciousness of the Violet Light in me moved me to develop the Master teaching of the Violet Light, now called: "The Master course of The Violet Light," which then became the third level and completed the teachings and the initiations.

Two years after The Violet Light

Two years later I went for a second aura reading with Thelma. I was impressed at the reading. According to her my aura showed a great spiritual evolution, the shape of it had dramatically changed. My aura had expanded three times its previous size. Thelma said that my karma overspill, what you have in excess, had gone from being over 35% to only 5%. That meant that I had to work 5% of karma off.

The reading also showed a great increase in the percentage of openness of my charkas. Those that were not very opened, were opened and some of the ones working properly, had opened more. This really means that more spiritual energy is going through them.

The Past

All this is amazing considering that violet was never my favorite color… that is until then. In fact I shied away from violet. Some time after the initiation, I recalled an episode that made me laugh then. I went to a session of color therapy many years before, that a lady was giving free of charge to get practice. So I went out of curiosity. I laid down on a kind of oriental bed surrounded with hanging garments and soft light. In relaxation, she put behind the neck of the person crystal tubes filled with liquids of different colors. She then asked what you felt with that specific color. At one point she put one of them behind my neck and I couldn't stand its energy. I said almost in shock: "I don't know what this is but take it away from me immediately!" It was the violet one.

The Announcement

The moment which was most amazing until Jesus came to give me the connection with the light, was in Paris six years before. A moment I have recently called "The Announcement." I was spending a relaxed weekend in Paris after assisting to a European meeting, representing the company I worked for as Marketing Director. As I walked about Paris that Saturday afternoon, I stopped by a fountain which I found very soothing and beautiful. I was enjoying the peaceful atmosphere produced by the sound of the water, when suddenly a violet light appeared over the water before me. It was like a rainbow, but this was a rather strange rainbow, it was only violet and had an unusual form. As soon as I could react, I took the camera out before that magical light of extraordinary beauty faded away. The picture came out very well. I treasured it since as a beautiful manifestation of the sunlight on water. Now that I understand what it was, I treasure it as the moment Heavens "told" me: *"The Violet Light is coming to your life."* You can see the photograph on the back cover.

As it happened at the time, I met a friend who lived in Paris and I spent most of the time with her. Her name happens to be "Violeta." Violet in Spanish.

Other light appearances

Two years after the Violet Light arrived, it started to appear in some of my photographs. Originally I wanted to print them here in the book, but for practical reasons it was not done. You can see them in my website. The Violet Light appeared first in a picture taken before leaving a restaurant in Mexico City, one evening. It showed as a beam of Violet Light on one side of the picture, literally floating in the air. Another one was half a moon of Violet and Gold light at ground level next to me, as I chopped wood near a lake.

The most outstanding is the one with an intensely brilliant ray of Violet Light, that appeared next to me as I was taken a picture watching a sunset in Isla Mujeres, an island off the coast of Cancun. One of the most recent appearances of the light in photographs, was in a village were I spend time writing, in a quiet region of Spain. One day I brought the Violet Light down on the town hall. I took some pictures of the village time after that, since I like the country atmosphere and the old houses. One of the pictures shows the bridge over the river and a part of the town hall house... with the Violet Light on it.

The place of initiation

The place where I received the Initiation was a room in the courtyard of a house, in Mexico City. In the middle of the courtyard there was a huge Jacaranda, a tree that gives out violet flowers. The violet flowers fell continually covering the ground with a violet carpet, that I had to walk through to enter my room. The tree was in front of my window, not far away from where I meditated. Nothing really surprising taking into account the continuous number of amazing "coincidences," surrounding the manifestation of the Violet Light.

It is not what it appears to be...

The day I was introducing in the book one of the most important parts of it, I found myself enveloped in a incredibly sweet field of Grace. It was one of the highest and most powerful experiences I have had. I went out to lunch. The energy was there with me. I was full of ecstasy and peace. As I observed the scene around me in that restaurant, the energy shifted my perception and then I saw a different scene. I saw that everybody was God, and that the game of life was to see how everyone was treating the God in the other... It was so amazing to see it, that I had to make a great effort to avoid breaking out with laughter in the middle of that place. It was so incredible to see the two sides at once: what appears to be, a restaurant full of people talking to each other, and what it really was, God experiencing life through everyone. I literally felt the Grace was ascending my perception as if it said to me: "Let me show you the view from a little higher up." And then I felt going up until I had that view of things. I can share with you that to see both sides of it made it so clear that this world is an illusion, and that we believe what is going on is "real" whereas it has nothing to do with what it is really about.

How my life changed

In my outer life things have taken a big turn. At the time, my housing situation changed from one extreme to the other, with tremendous improvements. I found a dream place in which to live, painted in violet, in front of a little forest with wonderful energy. My work situation improved extremely, as new projects started developing. New possibilities in all areas opened. My personal life at all levels experienced a take off. Since then I have experienced an expansion of all areas of my life. Generally all restrictions have gone.

I found myself amazed when I encountered certain situations in my life in which I knew how I would normally feel, and saw how different I was feeling and reacting. Even today I look back at many aspects of my personality, and I cannot stop offering my gratitude to God for all the wonderful changes through the influence of the Violet Light. Almost all negative reactions, conflictive feelings, and psychological blockages have gone. Most emotional unhappiness, negative emotions and fears have dissolved.

I experience more and more a greater unity with God. I feel Him so close and know from this how loving, benevolent and wonderful this consciousness we call God is. I see Him as the spark of life essence alive in everyone and in everything. This is a very expansive experience of life. I see that we are not personalities and we are not bound by physical bodies. We are life force of light, beyond birth and death. We move towards acquiring consciousness of that light essence. My intuition has expanded greatly and many wisdoms have developed in me. As time goes by I understand deeper and deeper what love is, and have more contact with and access to this Universal light force called The Violet Light.

•

The greatness of the light

My father was a very strong man with tremendous will power and self-control. Great qualities from which he deserves to be appreciated. On the other hand, he would never show his deep feelings, nothing that would have to do with supposed vulnerability. The last time we spoke in person, we had an intense confrontation after an incident which he blamed me for. I was going to live in another country the next day, so there was no time to allow things to settle. For almost two years he was not in touch with me. In that time I received the initiation of the Violet Light. Among the things I did with it, was to send Violet Light to him as a way of blessing him, making sure I gave him the best in me.

It was after those two years of my departure, when he wrote me a note in which he said he had not been feeling well since. He explained this was because of the situation we had, and that he wanted to apologize for he realized, I was not to blame for what had happened. I felt such relief for him that he finally had come to that openness of heart. He at last showed softness, tenderness. He could let go of his struggle. I thanked God immensely for this event and was so profoundly happy for my father. I had already forgiven him and had let go of the whole issue a long time before. I was glad because when he passed away few months later, I knew he left having released that from his heart. Finally he had opened his heart in a new way for him. It was one of the first times in which I became amazed at the power of the Violet Light.

When he passed away I sent him Violet Light many times. Years after a woman who connects with spiritual guides and beings beyond this plane of existence, said to me in a personal reading that my father was there and that had come to tell me a number of things. The first thing he said was: "Thank you for remembering me…"

CONCLUSION

*"I have all conviction because
all the power of God is with me."*
– Kahan

The presence of God manifested for me in this wonderful way – The Violet Light – when I asked with all my being. It happened when I gave myself completely to a greater experience, when I was prepared to received it all and then I opened my door completely. God then showed me what He had for me and for others.

Every day of my life I see the blessings of this light around me. My gratitude is immense and I cannot imagine what my life would be like without it. My life before the Violet Light, seems like a previous life. This is just a proof, of the many available, of what is here for you all if you want it.

I started the book saying that God has given us all, that we just need to find it, ask for it to be revealed. Then you open the door to it. It is all already there. It is the power of your love what will attract God to you, what will make Him fully available to you. This will reveal the infinite treasure within yourself. You will never do it with your mind. He is showing us the way of the heart. He is not interested in anything other than love. He will not be there. This is His teaching. You will only get God through love. This is the way to access His power, His love.

Ask God to unveil in you what you need. Do you need knowledge about something? Ask God to activate that knowledge in you. Do you need serenity? Ask for that revelation. He has the solution to all things; He has all the power. You just need to ask Him to install that program to work in you. Ask God, the Universal Source, The Great Spirit however you conceive Him to be, to install in you the activation of the "Divine Programs." You can make it happen.

I hope my experience inspires all of you to go for it.

*"And ye shall seek me,
and find me, when ye shall
search for me with all thy heart."*
– Jeremiah, 29:13

**"Dear God show me what you have given me.
Remove my veils of ignorance so that
I see, I recognize your gifts in me,
so that I use them for my blessing and
the blessing of others and of all life."**

Amen.

Common Concerns

I don't believe in God or Jesus. Can I benefit from The Violet Light? Is it right to do it if I don't believe.

The Violet Light is there the same way the sun is there. You do not need to believe in the sun or its light. You get its effects anyway. Spiritual light itself is independent of religions, faiths, beliefs or skepticism. The Violet Light will affect everybody independently of their beliefs. It is like water. You get wet from contact with it. It is not a mind thing. The light is the same. It just is. And as you get within its influence you will receive the benefits. It is like sunlight, you get its benefits just by being under it. It is right you do it. The light will not ask for conditions.

Could the light create situations of crisis if you are not well?

The Violet Light takes care of everything – itself. It is Divine Intelligence. It could at some point bring a condition to a healing crisis, but even that is a liberating one and a freeing experience. Purification. When it happens like that, it is because it speeds up the process, so you become free faster. And you have those years it would have taken you to solve all that, free to really advance.

Also you can use the Golden Light at any moment to stabilize energies, the mind, the emotions, or the body itself, or mix periods of Golden Light within the work of the Violet Light. You do it with the same techniques used for the Violet Light. Just change it to Gold.

I am very sensitive to negative energies. How can I protect myself?

The Violet Light protects you. When you exist in a higher vibration, lower vibrations don't affect you. This is the general rule. You will certainly feel them faster and will be able to keep away from them. Your own high vibration will make them bounce back or it will transmute them. This sometimes takes work and what often happens is that your aura and energy field will burn these energies. Although you must know that for a short time they can make you feel uncomfortable, depending on your sensitivity and energy management. But with your meditation and focusing on surrounding yourself with Violet Light, you will release any low frequencies that bother you or that get stuck to you.

This happens all the time with everyone. Just that they are generally not aware. As you become more and more aware, you will know what is happening in your aura and you will be able to do something positive about it, relinquishing the hindrance of having low frequency energies stuck to you without noticing it.

You can visualize circles of Violet Light around your wrists, ankles and head, as well as around your aura. As you meditate more and more on the Violet Light you will become stronger, your Violet energy field will protect you. But it takes time. Just know that you need to keep working and advancing in your understanding and learning, as to how to deal with them whenever you feel uncomfortable and bothered by energies. Have faith, the light protects you.

"I know the Violet Flame, I already work with this energy. What is different?

The flame is a form of the Light, a manifestation of it. Everything works in cycles – superior ascending cycles. Now the Violet Light has an increased power, it comes with greater intensity. It brings new frequencies we never had before. We never had all the power of the Violet Light, it would have been too much for the way things were.

Also the way it works is very different. In the past, it was necessary to spend a great deal of time pronouncing decrees. That has been the main way to work with the Violet Flame. Now you don't have to open your mouth at all. The way it comes through this source is direct, it reaches you with all the power just because you are there.

Spirit is also evolving. Creation is not set and that is it, it is evolving. This is a new form of the light that comes from Spirit, from God as we need it now. Otherwise it wouldn't be here. You wouldn't want to have a car from fifty years back for the needs of today's life. You would want the latest. This is the same. We have the latest design and engineering of the Violet Light as created by God Source, for the Universe and the Earth. It is greater than before, it has been improved, enhanced, its power is greater, its love more infinite even than before, and its effectiveness is totally new for us.

I have a spiritual Master. How does this teaching fit into it? If I do Violet Light, do I have to leave him?

Don't change your path – your religion. It is your treasure. Just add Violet Light to it. It will increase the frequencies of your spiritual work, which no doubt are already very high. It is the nature of the vibration of this light, that takes all particles of energy and matter and increases their resonance. So go for it and see what it does for you. Take it as a great support from God which is available to you now. The light does not belong to any path. It is spiritual light.

Can I not access the Violet Light directly and do it all that way?

Of course you can. But as it has always happened in the world, there have been people that have mastered the connection with light and Grace, like Jesus and then other people received it from them. Now it is the same. Grace and liberation have always been available, mostly through real hard work, but most people have been lost not knowing the way. So if you are trying to get higher, make your life work better, become more enlightened, why don't you get it from someone who can bring it down for you instantly? You sure are working at it, but sometimes it is very much like hammering a rock and not much seems to happen. Why do you think Jesus came here for? If people were doing it fast enough and in great numbers, he wouldn't have needed to come. I speak as if he is still here because he is, although not visible most of the time. Also we wouldn't need other great spiritual masters that we have in the world now. But to cross the Himalayas you need a good guide, or else you could never find your way out of there. People easily accept guidance and help in worldly matters, like financial advice, or doctor's guidance. If you want to be a doctor, you accept the teachings of doctors. But when it comes to spirituality many want to do it on their own, and there are many people confused as a result of it. Why would they in the area most subtle, and in the one in which they can get really lost, want to do it without a guide? If you find your way, fine. If you don't, get expert help. If you can do it on your own try this anyway, sure you will find it a lot easier with the connection provided here. It is very immediate and very deep. It is just the way it is. The important thing is not to let the ego enter into our spiritual decisions, and to be open to use what is available for us.

But we are our own masters... aren't we?

The point is to get help, to receive a true spiritual activation like this one or the many true ones that are around. Then learn to walk with it, meditate on it, discover what has been given to you, learn form the Master there and from people more advanced. Once your connection with your own divine source is strong, you don't need any guides because your own inner Master and guide is fully activated and it guides you. But to go alone before that point, is a challenge that has many wondering how to advance more and really being unable to do it. This is because you have to cross the treacherous lands of the kingdom of the ego, and they are filled with delusion and many traps that are not easily recognizable – unless your spiritual energy is strong and your consciousness very awakened.

I have seen this in many people and continue to see it. The ego is the worst enemy; it is the devil itself. If you are not trained, prepared to face it, it will get the best of you every time. You have to be prepared to deal with this energy. Like a samurai warrior, or a martial arts Master that confront their very able enemies who know all the tricks and secret movements and techniques, and that can always surprise the unprepared. But many people today are in those traps and don't get out because they don't recognize they are in. More light is necessary. The value of help in this spiritual energy is enormous. Here we are talking about initiation: spiritual activation. This means that your spiritual energy is activated at whatever level it is now. It is a transmission of spiritual power that comes from the Divine Source. That activates your own spiritual energy permanently. Direct, awakened connection with God is where we are all going towards in this new era. Sai Baba once said to me internally in a Dharsan in his ashram in India: "The purpose of a Master is to take you to your divine source. Once you arrive there you go to it to drink directly from that source." Then you embrace your spiritual independence, when that source is very active, when you know the way there by heart and in a storm and with your eyes closed or open – literally – then and only then, you can call yourself spiritually independent: your own Master. People have to realize that the purpose of a true Master, is to guide them to that divine source inside, not to have permanent disciples. And it is often not that a Master cares , it is that disciples want to be disciples forever!

The Violet Light takes you to your divine source, so you can experience the Grace of God inside you. So ultimately this is a choice you have. You can have what is given here, or you can pass on it. You are the sovereign of your decisions.

What about intermediaries to get to God? You talk about spiritual independence. Doesn't this teaching make you dependent?

Jesus himself brought Grace, initiation but he was a bridge between Man and God. He taught to worship God not the bridge. His presence was so necessary for humanity because of the state in which it was. Now again, the presence of people directly connected to Grace, is very much a great need in the world. There is a need for people directly connected with Grace that can connect others quickly; we need many bridges doing that. The bridge is necessary to a point, but when you cross it you don't need it any more. A bridge is a function to restore something to its original state, it is temporary, it gives you a connection to make you independent. An intermediary is an agent that acts on behalf of, and makes you dependent on it. It provides a permanent service. Its subsistence depends on being a permanent presence between you and God. An intermediary makes you dependent. A bridge makes you independent.

I took the course of the Violet Light and since then some of my friends are not in touch any more. Some have reacted with strong rejection towards me and I have not said anything about the light.

The Violet Light is a very challenging power. Lower vibrations can't compete with it. Darkness dissolves before its high frequency. Ego doesn't stand a chance, so it retaliates and recedes. The dark ego side in people fights the light in an attempt to keep its existence. This energy is very powerful, the light will make the ego die, dissolve. So as you are near some people with this vibration, their subconscious negative egos will be challenged because the high frequencies of the light are hitting them. Then the ego reacts and some people cannot handle that, so they reject you as the bringer of that vibration. That part of their psyche doesn't want to be near that vibration. Other people with more light and consciousness will come to you. Probably you are finding that too. Some vibrations are not compatible. Those relationships have served their purpose. If you are with this light whatever is gone, is gone. Most probably those relationships were not based on truth. I am sure if you are honest with yourself and look into it, most probably you will find that. The light evolves situations dissolving from existence what is not appropriate. Be happy. Greater realities are on the way.

Do we have the right to send Violet Light or light energy to people?

It is not your will you are invoking or putting there, but the Will of God. Do not fear, do not worry about this. You are using a divine instrument, an instrument of God to bless everyone. Do not let negativity in the form of doubt enter you. It often takes the form of "well, do I really have the right to do this for that person? Or "should I not ask for permission first?" or any of the kind. You are asking God to manifest fully for the greater good of a person or a situation. That is all you are doing. When you pray for someone, do you question whether you have the right to ask for help? You don't. You are asking God to intervene and feel this is right. It is. This is the same. Sending Violet Light to people is to send blessings: asking God to intervene. By the power granted to you in the Violet Light here, you are a channel of God and therefore of His Grace. That blesses people.

I have been meditating for 25 years after I received a spiritual initiation, with advanced spiritual states. Do I need this light?

You don't need it as such. What is interesting is to appreciate what it can do for you at this point. Your case is quite common. People from many religious and spiritual backgrounds with many years of advanced experience, have approached the teachings and have received the light. It has been very welcomed by them. They have been able to recognize that there was something valuable for them and their lives in it, partly because they had that background. All of the ones who have mentioned their experience afterwards, have been extremely happy for having this light connection. They have spoken wonders of the Violet Light and have appreciated what it has done for them. It is useful to look at it from this perspective, and to see it in terms of what the Violet Light can add to your experience with its gifts. It has been the case with many, and with myself, that the light has made all the spiritual gifts or achievements already there blossom further. In a word, it will accelerate your evolutional process and expand your light.

I have read books that speak about the spiritual experience and the deep love experience, and explain those concepts. I understand them and then I follow what they say in my meditation. But I don't seem to get very far into it. It is as if the door is closed.

The thing is that you cannot use the mind to go into the heart. You cannot have the experience of the heart from the mind. To experience the heart, you have to go to the heart and leave the mind. You have to take a jump, dive from the mind into the heart. But you leave the mind behind. A great number of books are excellent with their explanations, and approach the subject the right way. A lot of people, and books, and teachings might talk about the heart experience. But some just talk about it. They excel in the understanding of it, missing the whole point: it is not about intellect, it is about experience. You need to understand in your mind to a point, but then leave it all behind and go for it. The understanding is necessary as a map. But then you need the experience, and it is the experience that will give you the true understanding. Much intellectual understanding of the experience of love, will not make you or anyone experience a fraction of what love is. Far from it, it becomes a hindrance, because you are full of ideas about it and they do not let you embrace the immediacy of the experience directly. Like understanding how a delicious gourmet dish is made, will not give you the experience. And to experience it you do not need to use your mind. The experience is not in concepts. It is not an intellectual thing. You reach God and that level of love by getting out of the mind and entering the heart. I have seen this happening to many people and they go around in circles, with great intellectual understanding and little experience.

The bottle has to open at a certain place at a certain point, for you to drink the water inside. Looking at it forever will just kill you of thirst. I have joined in spiritual practices and meditations where there wasn't a heart experience. There was a very dry energy; it was like the honey was missing from the recipe. The sweetness wasn't there. This is what happens when you try to do it from the mind. There is no surrender of it to the heart. The heart has to take over; this is surrender. It is not about intellectual pursue to conquer the heart and the divine experience there, by figuring out with the mind how to get to it. People try to use the mind as a can-opener for everything and also for the heart. That doesn't work. What is required is that all is dropped. So it means to surrender all and to come before the heart naked, which is to come before God naked. No self-importance that you are going to do it, and that you know how to, and if you don't, you think that you will crack it at some point. You will crack eventually that way. That will be good because it will be the way you will do it. That cracking will bring you to humility and in that openness, you will start experiencing those sweet and melting qualities of love that everyone is looking for. Techniques, ideas, concepts are part of your own agenda. The attitude there is: "I have it. Now I know how to do it. I'll try this and it will work this time."

You are wasting your time. You cannot go into the heart with your ways. You cannot go into the heart through a side door – an idea or technique you just found. There will be enlightened techniques that will help you get ready to enter the front door, but not to get around it. Techniques that work, have Grace or invoke it. Techniques are a method. The key thing is the Grace connection. Then the techniques serve to guide you, to focus your mind, to shape you in different ways with the Grace. There is no side door. There is just front door and you have to be prepared to face it. This will mean facing yourself and your dark areas, and all that you don't want to see about yourself; then it will mean being true to yourself: no manipulation. There are no short cuts that will make you avoid you going through facing your truth. It won't happen for you then. You have to be very honest with God and the heart. You will not do it your way; you will do it the heart's way.

God in the heart knows the secret code that opens the door. And using the mind and the intellect does not have the secret combination to do it. You come with your agenda and you are spotted right away. So you are not allowed in: the wisdom of the heart is greater. You are bringing to the heart's sacred realm things that cannot survive in the sacred atmosphere of the heart. So you are not allowed in. You have to have the secret code: surrender. That opens the door. So leave the mind aside and go into the heart empty, humble This might take you some practice until you understand what it is about. But you are now moving in the right direction. The good thing about using the Violet Light is that it does not care at all for your mind or ego, and with its love, it will melt them away, so it is making you ready to be where you have to be for that deep divine experience. It is one of the sweetest and most powerful experiences you will ever have.

So ask yourself what you want: do you want the recipe or do you want the dish?

You have explained in this talk the vision of the Violet Light, and how it transforms people and situations just by touching them. It sounds too easy...

Many people have "buts" about the workings of God. I acknowledge that we are not used to the experience of Grace, at least not in a big way. This is obvious looking at the state of the world. A great deal of people do experience it though, and live connected with Grace. But for many this is not even a reality they would believe in or contemplate – even if it was next to them. We live life quite disconnected from God, and humanity has got into this state of affairs through a great massive disconnection from God Source. This includes being disconnected from His powers. But we do not have to do anything to deserve Grace. We just have to open the door. You are talking from a place that doubts or ignores His power. So from that perspective it sounds too easy. If God is all power, what is difficult for Him?

God vibrates and creates; He just wills and things happen. So He makes things happen when He is there. So yes, it is very easy because it is Him who does it. It is very easy for the power of God in whatever form it comes, to make anything happen. It is like using a very advanced technology from across the Universe that is unknown to humans. Maybe for the first time in your life, you are being faced with this possibility: that good things can happen to you from an apparently outside force, without your intervention. That sounds like the perfect definition of Grace. It is. What we are talking about here is precisely Grace. At this point in your life, knowing this you have the option of accepting it, to accept that this is a reality and that it is here before you.

But the only way you are going to find out that it works this way, is by having the experience. You will never discover it thinking about it with your mind. You won't figure it out. You can only find and see for yourself how easy it really is, by being touched by the light.

I wonder if it is for me... Should I be more advanced? I don't think I am prepared.

What is your true concern really? What is it you are doubting? Maybe you don't feel you deserve it, or you may have some fears.

We really live in a world devoid of the experience of Grace. That has created a distorted psychology that considers things are hard and you need to be qualified. And that of course takes years, hard work and discipline. Of course, this is a world that has a very bad relationship with God. It hardly knows Him. There is the collective unconscious vision that things are slow, hard and that you have to work hard and suffer for a long time, to achieve anything worthwhile. And then you have to prove your achievement. Then you feel great and everybody thinks you are really worth something. Now let me ask you this: how much hard work do you think it took God to create the Universe, from the smallest cell to the greatest galaxy and beyond? Do you think He is prepared? And what qualifications would He need for that? Yes, the issue is mind blowing. It is just beyond you and me.

With the Violet Light, you don't have to understand deep spiritual matters. You don't need any qualifications to receive the Grace of God. Otherwise it would not be Grace. What qualifications, or experience, or readiness do you need to sunbathe? It just happens. Does it depend on you? So what qualifications do you need to receive the Grace of God? It just happens. Does it depend on you? This is an idea of the ego that thinks it has some control, and therefore by qualifying it thinks it has more power. Training is what is necessary: training of the mind in the right direction – training in seeing the truth, to become free from illusion. But the extremely unbalanced occidental culture wants you to be so qualified these days in order to let you do anything, that people are loosing perspective. Qualifying spiritually does not happen in the ego, and no ego qualifications will get you nearer to God. Qualification is in the soul, and it is already there. The question should really be: "Am I ready to accept it?" "Do I feel I deserve it?" And that I cannot answer. Like with healing, it happens with faith, prayer, meditations... through Grace. And still modern medicine and its keepers want to disqualify it as illusion or fake – anything rather than accept the power and presence of God, and the fact that they do not have all the answers. The healing is there... "but you are not qualify as a doctor" well, who is qualifying you to say that? and deciding you have that "power." In this distorted view someone could go to a flower and ask: "Well, God did you do that? Are you qualified?" Isn't that enough proof? The flower is there... so that is the qualification with God. You know why there is so much need for proving people can do certain things that depend on their inner power? because the system is ruled by individuals that have lost their connection with that power. I can show you a paper that says: "Certified to do this work, by

God" – beautiful gold letters on violet paper… and then you sit in the course and nothing happens to you. You go home. They ask you: "How was it?" "Well… I didn't feel anything really, but the guy is qualified, you know." Is that how we want to be? Let's move away from the mind and enter into reality. Qualifications are fine in the realm of the world. In the realm of spirit, God's power rules. So with Grace you don't need to be ready or qualified to receive it. The only requirement to sunbathe is that you are under the sunlight. With Grace it is the same, you just need to be under it to receive it.

You want God? You are prepared.

When you change with the Violet Light, can you go back to where you were before?

This is alchemy. It means transformation. It is a metamorphosis – a butterfly cannot go back to the worm it came from. It is a different state. Glass comes from sand. Once you have the glass, you cannot go back to the sand. This is the same. Fire transmutes sand into glass. This energy is Divine Fire: it transmutes people into higher beings. Such is the action of God's love; it is the alchemy of God's love. The previous states of the process just fall out of existence.

What you have to do is work at exposing yourself to the frequencies of light in meditation, so that the mind does not repeat the same patterns. The mind is like metal, it keeps the memory of a contact after what produced the shape in it, is gone. So the memory in the mind will have the tendency to recreate the pattern. Meditation will help to avoid this and will reshape the mind.

Who are the Ascended Masters?

This is not a mystical question I want to clarify. This is a very basic question. We are all Ascended Masters in potential. So they are the individuals that through their communion with Spirit, have become one with It and in that transmutation have accessed all the love, power and wisdom of that Spirit Source. In that communion, they have moved completely away from identification with ego or ego realities as what they are, and have recognized, by being it, their own divine identity. Examples are Jesus, Buddha, Saint Germain, Kuan Yin, Lady Nada, and many more from other spiritual traditions. Also there are many unknown that have done the same, but that are not identified in the spiritual traditions of the world. So you can also become an Ascended Master. This is where we are going. Eventually everyone will have to be ascended. The present state of consciousness is not normal. It is below normal. We are not on the surface level yet as humanity. We are well below what we are in terms of consciousness. When we see and identify God in everything as the reality of all life, we will really begin. We are in a descended state now. By ascending we become what we are.

God is everything light, dark...good and bad. God is both. He created all. Why reject the dark?

There are a lot of misconceptions about God. God is not darkness, God is light. Absence of Him is darkness, but He doesn't create it. We do. We are in duality. He is Oneness. From duality we think in separation, and see Him from our dualistic perspective. He is not that. If He was light and darkness there would be separation there, and there is no separation in God. Where there is light, darkness is not. If He is all light, He cannot be darkness; that light He is melts all darkness. You cannot have both together they are mutually exclusive. The sun is light; it casts darkness because something blocks its light. That creates separation. If nothing blocks light, you have only light. But we are blocking God with our contraction, ignorance, fear, in a word separation. We block God's light and we think He creates the resulting darkness. No He doesn't. We stand on the way of His light and cast a shadow. The Violet Light dissolves the action of blocking God's light so that we access it more directly.

This level of existence separates light from dark to create a contrast and to gain consciousness. It is an evolutional place. Light does not manifest fully here. It can be condensed as matter and then it blocks finer light. It is a game of light that creates the illusion we live in: this apparent world. It is a matrix – a hologram – created by densities of light and their interplay. Everything is light. But it is crystallized, so we see a sofa and think: "that is a sofa." Well, it is dense light. But it appears as a sofa at this level of perception. Since the sofa is crystallized energy, it blocks light and then it casts a shadow. So duality is born. I remember while I lived in England, often I looked at the sea near where I lived. Many times I saw the sea becoming light before my eyes. Through the high spiritual energy and intense meditation of that time, I could tap into the reality of it: the light where it came from.

The Violet Light breaks dawn solidified light liberating consciousness trapped in form. For us this means that our consciousness is released from the constrictions of that crystallization of form, so it can return to spirit consciousness recovering all the power, freedom, love and joy that this entails.

Darkness... it needs to be embraced, turning the light on it. But don't stay there as if it is a place to be, or have it in your house as a guest.

What about our own darkness?

We have parts that are not in the light. We reject them, become "puritan" and see the evil in our brothers. Then we can't stand that darkness and want to get rid of it. So we start fighting our neighbor. In a big scale it is when a country starts throwing bombs on another, or when someone starts a war in the name of religion because they are "saints" and the others are the "evil ones." What is happening is that we can't stand the sight of darkness outside of us because it reminds us of our own darkness, which is repressed. We have to look at our own darkness, that which is not so saintly in us and recognize it, embrace it. We have to bring our darkness to the light. Keeping it hidden does not solve it. It is repression and that is a time bomb. Repressed consciousness will always push for recognition. If not integrated, the dark side will posses you – like Dr. Jeckill and Mr. Hyde. Consciousness is whole; you cannot fragment it and not suffer. You cannot fragment it and expect things to be resolved. We have to open up to our dark side and become conscious of it, then embrace it. To bring it to our awareness is to bring it to the light.

As we meditate, dark issues are more and more brought to the light and as we acknowledge them, they are resolved. Then we are healed and we become more conscious and loving.

What about God? Father God, Mother God.

We might think that God is Mother and Father. He is not, He is. That is all. When God manifests in form, He moves out of formlessness and manifests different parts. Those are the Yin and Yang forces, feminine and masculine principles that originate gender: woman and man and the dual world we know. But let's remember we live in a dual world, opposites that complement each other. Beyond that, in the realms of Spirit everything is oneness; God is oneness. He doesn't act with a human mind, He is Universal. With the human mind we create concepts. Then we have a perception through those filters and believe that is the Truth. It is not. It is only our perception. And through that we read God as mother and father. Our perception depends on our human perspective. When we recover our divine perspective, we see and understand Him and all... as oneness.

If one receives the Violet Light, does it depend on the blockages one has as to how much of it one gets?

What you get doesn't depend on anything. It will happen wherever you are in yourself. The light will take you to the next step for you. If you had strong emotional blockages, the next step for you would be to be free from them. This is what the Violet Light will transmute in you first, in that case. Once it has removed your blockages, you will be more open to experience happiness and joy as your natural states. But this is a process. I am giving the basics here. Do not think that because the light is so powerful and helpful, that you will see heaven from one day to the next. It will burn so much density from you... you might never know what it did to you, but you will know eventually something major has shifted. And you have to do your work. The Violet Light does wonders in you. But it puts you to work.

I am a doctor. I have three children. How can the Violet Light change my life or help me?

With it you will function with resources beyond your mind, resources of the spirit. This is more efficient and liberating. They are unlimited. Your life is not going to change, meaning you are still going to be mother, have a job and a busy life. What is going to change is your experience of it and how you deal with it. With the Violet Light your inner soul power will be activated. Your higher power and love, what I call "love power." This means you will have all your inner resources available for your outer life. The difference this will make is comparable to using batteries or using a connection to main power. In practical terms, you will be empowered in a new way to deal with all aspects of your life. When this divine power manifests permanently in you, you will be able to function with greater fluidity in all areas of your life; stress and tension will have gone from you, if they were there. You will experience a peace inside that will carry you through all the events of your life. Your higher luminosity will bring greater wisdom and love to all around you, and you will be a greater agent for progress, harmony and understanding. You will find that everything moves forward in the right direction with almost no effort, and that things just seem to happen naturally in the appropriate manner for you, without having to think hard about it. Those little problems that always seem to make things more difficult, and at the end of the day wear you out day in and day out, will have disappeared. Your energy will be less edgy and more supportive and loving, even than what is now. You will not have the sensation that you are rushing to get all done by the end of the day, and that this is all in life. Your family and patients will feel this and receive its benefit too. You will be able to help others much more with your own energy, through the empowerment of the Violet Light. Then you will develop a greater sense of communion with life, others and the Universe since you will feel a power greater than you that supports you always. As that happens, you will find that the small issues are not so important. You won't be so bothered by them. You will feel the relativity of life here, as your consciousness expands to embrace and commune with the eternal in you. Just existing will fill you with joy. You will understand that life is not about being a doctor or a mother, those are your roles now, but about being in the right place at the right time, fulfilling your mission and serving the Universe. This standpoint will give you a detachment and a liberation, from where to understand your life and your roles with a greater perspective. As you move ahead, you will understand that you are serving a greater purpose and you will experience the bliss of freedom.

I find things are going very fast. Time is going very fast; I don't have time to do everything. Can you explain what is happening?

These times are very fast. The acceleration of frequencies on the planet compresses everything and time is also affected. So time seems shorter than before. The same amount of time now is less, so we cannot do the same things we did with it before. This makes us live our lives in a different way. What do you do when you have many things and not enough time? You set priorities. So it forces us to define what really is important in our lives. The spiritual realities of life and our own spiritual evolution, acquire a new focus. Those are the most important things in our lives and we need to give them that place. We need to actively do something for our spiritual evolution. People at large are awakening from a deep sleep. Finally a great amount of people in humanity are seriously realizing that this can't be it. This is not a normal way to live. So this acceleration is putting "consciousness development" at the top of the list for a great number of people. We have the feeling there is no time: "I have to do so many things." We have to learn how not to become involved with everything; we have to make choices and select, then let the less important things go. We all have to drop things and we have to understand there is only time for the essential. When you go too fast, it means you are getting too busy. Go back to simplicity.

I find that I am getting anxious and pressurized with the time changes. What can I do? "

There are many changes happening inside and we need to take care of ourselves in the proper way. This often is in a new way. When you feel it is too much, go to a quiet place for two days, find your center again. We are learning in our psyche and in the body, to accommodate the new frequencies. During those periods, work in shorter spans of time. Rest, meditate. Make sure you go into Nature as much as possible. Don't go faster than what your body can handle. Take time every day to find your center. Go to a quiet place and there meditate, pray. Breathe deeply and calm yourself this way, calm your mind and your body. Priority is that you are well and function properly to be able to accomplish your tasks, while you are centered and at peace. The energies on the planet are new and we need to learn how to function in them. Don't let pressure set in. It is not the way we should go. I know it seems there is so much going on that you need to accelerate the way you go about things, and then you can't go that fast, so you feel you are going crazy. Peace is what is important, not doing things. So don't lose perspective. Don't lose your peace. Treasure it, it is your most valuable possession. Make of it your state of existence, your way of existing. In the middle of it all, stop the pressure to fulfill a role. Do not try to be anything; stop wanting to be something. Let it all happen naturally. Do the right work without controlling desire. Be egoless. Get out of the way and let Grace fill you and fulfill you, and lead you. Listen to your inner voice; it is guiding you.

●

FINAL WORD

Whenever you feel lonely or are going through difficult times, go to the Violet Light as you have learnt here – it is your best ally – and remember you are not alone. The Masters are with you, the presence of God is with you, I am with you. We all support you because you want to grow and be well, find peace and experience love. You, like me and all want freedom from bondage and suffering, and it is the will of all the spiritual lineage I represent through this work, that you are free and merge with limitless and unconditional love, the only place of true peace. This is why we are here, why the presence of the Violet Light is here with us, and why I wrote this book. I wrote it for you and for all like you, to find a new form of freedom, peace, spiritual growth, a new form of love power. Praying works. Invoking God works. Using the Violet Light works. You just have to do it. Open the door and your heart to divine communication and assistance. From now on we can all be with the Masters and the Violet Light inside, in the regions of Spirit, the home of all in the Divine Father Source.

From the center of my heart and soul, blessings of Violet Light to all.

Amen.

Contact the teachings

Kahan gives live initiations on The Violet Light in courses and workshops. He also gives courses on ascension and personal power. See information below and visit our website.

The Teachings of the Violet Light

Base Course
One day. Main teaching. Overview of The Violet Light. Main Activation. It is essentially the Course of The Violet Light contained in this book. The spiritual energy present in this teaching is very potent and penetrating, as well as loving, embracing and uplifting.

Transmutation Workshop
Two days. It helps you liberate all burdens from the past, to be born anew to life with greater clarity, consciousness and love power. Very practical course for the transmutation of all aspects of life: past lives, subconscious, birth, death. It includes structures of light, advanced techniques; temple of The Violet Light. It contains the second initiation and a new chakra teaching. It provides a very profound and sweet experience of the Higher Self. The energy in this workshop is a very deep and sweet soothing Grace. It is an irresistible melting experience of deep love.

Master Course of The Violet Light
Two days. How to be a Master in life from the perspective and consciousness of The Violet Light. Mastery of life is reviewed in depth through many teachings and meditations. It contains the Master Activation of The Violet Light. In it you are invested with the Master vibration of The Violet Light. This course increases your light and vibration dramatically. Your divine connection is enhanced profoundly, all resulting in a greater mastery over yourself and life.

After this course you can teach and impart activations if you wish. The energy of Grace here is very strong.

See website for full programs and details.

Requirements

There are no requirements to take the Base Course or The Transmutation Workshop. For the Master Course of The Violet Light, the other two are a must.

We bring the teachings to you

If you want Kahan to give The Violet Light live courses in your area, please send en e-mail with the heading: **"We want the teachings"** explaining details. Take into account that there must be sufficient people for us to travel. See website for e-mail.

Meditation groups

You can create working and meditation groups based on The Violet Light teachings. Visit our website for details. Also you can create planetary meditation groups to help create global peace and ascension. Also see the website. If you have created a meditation group or want to create one, let us know so we can support you. Send an e-mail with the heading: **"We have a meditation group."**

Experiences & Gratitude

We welcome experiences of The Violet Light for reference and further teachings. Also you may express your gratitude with them. If you want to share experiences, make sure they are relevant to others and contain transforming material. They should not be more than half a page. Put in the heading of your e-mail: **"Experiences to share."** Tell us basic facts about yourself, like name, profession. If you do not want your name to be used with the experience, say so in your e-mail. We thank you deeply in advance for your contribution.

There is also music played by Kahan that has the vibration of The Violet Light. It is now available. It has been played over the years in The Violet Light live courses. You can listen to it while doing the activation meditations. See website for details.

Next book: **"Flying Within"** – a powerful spiritual novel. Go to the website for details.

We cannot enter into individual consultation or correspondence for obvious reasons. All is contained here. Beyond that, go to your inner temple of light in the heart and trust the guidance of your Luminous Self.

Namaste.

Website: www.violetplatinum.com

About the author

Paco Alarcon – Kahan, has been involved in oriental and occidental spiritual currents for more than twenty years. As a result of his deep implication he acquired a strong connection with spiritual energy, gaining access to great spiritual revelations. From them he developed a number of original teachings, to bring spiritual energy and its power to people's lives. He created a wide range of courses to provide a new and deep understanding of the spiritual nature of Man in an innovative way, making spiritual experiences very accessible. His teachings reveal all the potency and depth of the spiritual realities, bringing people closer to the real experience of God. He aims at uniting the power of Spirit with the day to day life. He has worked in several countries and published many articles on spiritual growth. He also had his own mystical column in one of the leading newspapers of Mexico. He is also a spiritual counselor and spends great part of his time traveling, giving conferences and courses. He has written three books on personal spiritual growth, and is working on a book about recovering personal power as the way to spiritual ascension.

CPSIA information can be obtained
at www.ICGtesting.com
Printed in the USA
BVOW08s0721260317
479466BV00001B/134/P

9 781418 450298